THE ROYAL AIR FORCE IN TEXAS

Best Wishes

Tom Killebrew

War and the Southwest Series

Series editors:
Richard G. Lowe, Gustav L. Seligmann, Calvin L. Christman

The University of North Texas Press has undertaken to publish a series of significant books about War and the Southwest. This broad category includes first-hand accounts of military experiences by men and women of the Southwest, histories of warfare involving the people of the Southwest, and analyses of military life in the Southwest itself. The Southwest is defined loosely as those states of the United States west of the Mississippi River and south of a line from San Francisco to St. Louis as well as the borderlands straddling the Mexico-United States boundary. The series includes works involving military life in peacetime in addition to books on warfare itself. It ranges chronologically from the first contact between indigenous tribes and Europeans to the present. The series is based on the belief that warfare is an important if unfortunate fact of life in human history and that understanding war is a requirement for a full understanding of the American past.

Books in the series:

FOO—A Japanese-American Prisoner of the Rising Sun

Wen Bon: A Naval Air Intelligence Officer behind Japanese Lines in China in WWII

An Artist at War: The Journal of John Gaitha Browning

The 56th Evac Hospital: Letters of a WWII Army Doctor

CAP Môt: The Story of a Marine Special Forces Unit in Vietnam, 1968-1969

"Surrounded by Dangers of all Kinds": The Mexican War Letters of Lieutenant Theodore Laidley

Crossing the Pond: The Native American Effort in World War II

THE ROYAL AIR FORCE IN TEXAS

● ●

TRAINING BRITISH PILOTS IN TERRELL DURING WORLD WAR II

TOM KILLEBREW

Foreword by Air Vice-Marshal H. Gill, CB, OBE

Number Eight in the War and the Southwest Series

University of North Texas Press
Denton, Texas

10 9 8 7 6 5 4 3 2

Permissions:
University of North Texas Press
1155 Union Circle #311336
Denton, TX 76203-5017

The paper used in this book meets the minimum requirements of the American National Standard for Permanence of Paper for Printed Library Materials,
z39.48.1984. Binding materials have been chosen for durability.

Library of Congress Cataloging-in-Publication Data
Killebrew, Tom.
  The Royal Air Force in Texas : training British pilots in Terrell during World
War II / Tom Killebrew ; foreword by Air Vice-Marshal H. Gill.
      p. cm. — (War and the Southwest series ; no. 8)
Includes bibliographical references and index.
  ISBN 1-57441-169-1 (cloth : alk. paper)
  ISBN-13 978-1-57441-272-7 (paper : alk. paper)
  1. No. 1 British Flying Training School—History. 2. Great Britain. Royal Air
Force—Foreign service—Texas. 3. Aeronautics, Military—Study and teach-
ing—Great Britain. 4. Aeronautics, Military—Study and teaching—Texas—
Terrell. 5. Terrell (Tex.)—History, Military—20th century. I. Title. II. Series.
  UG639.G72 T475 2003
  940.54'4941'09764922—dc21
                            2003009983

The Royal Air Force in Texas: Training British Pilots in Terrell during World War II is
Number Eight in the War and the Southwest Series

Design by Angela Schmitt

To Ann
and
the young men of the Royal Air Force
who journeyed so far

And the king said unto me. . . .
For how long shall thy journey be?
and when wilt thou return?

Nehemiah 2:6

CONTENTS

Illustrations following page 102:

FOREWORD

As a product of the British Flying Training School enterprise, I am delighted to have an opportunity to write the foreword to this splendid and intimate record of its unique history.

In 1939, Britain and its Empire resolved to fight against the threat of European and world domination by Hitler's Nazi Germany. Early studies showed that whereas raw and manufactured materials necessary to sustain a vastly accelerated aircraft production programme might be viable, training facilities to provide the correspondingly increased number of Royal Air Force aircrew would be the greater problem. The skies above Britain were already overcrowded with rising operational activity. Grass airfields and agricultural land were giving way to a massive and urgent programme of airfield construction including concrete runways, and at night, Britain was in darkness. From early discussions, to which officers from the United States Army Air Corps were party, adequacy of the British Empire Training Scheme that provided flying training facilities in Canada, Rhodesia, and South Africa was questioned. Although at that early stage the United States had not entered the war, proposals for similar flying training facilities in the United States were generously offered, accepted and installed by mid-1941 as British Flying Training Schools.

The BFTS system worked swiftly and well. Selected as a potential pilot, a young man underwent brief elementary training in Britain up to solo stage, a fast ocean liner voyage from Scotland to Canada, and then a long train journey south. The temperature change, sometimes severe, was absorbed beneath the excitement of what for many was a first journey overseas. Upon arrival at the BFTS, the forms of welcome varied, but all were very touching and often emotional. Beyond that, cadets were swiftly taken into the hearts, minds, and homes of local people who extended the warmest hands of friendship imaginable. Arriving as young 18- or 19-year-olds from a land at war, where most commodities were strictly rationed, we found ourselves in one where we were spontaneously and thoroughly spoiled. With regard to training, the civilian flying instructors were first class, friendly to a point which did not inhibit the effectiveness of their tuition, "hell" if it was necessary, or a pat on the shoulder for doing well.

The overall and ultimate contribution made by the BFTS scheme to the successful prosecution of the war in Europe and beyond is incalculable. In retrospect, all of this reflected the warmth and durability of the long-standing cooperation and friendship at the international level between Britain and America, which then existed and which prevails today. I cannot foresee a future where this would not be so.

For those who can cast their minds back to these momentous days, as well as for those who cannot, this lively and historic account represents compelling reading and I commend it to all ages, young and old alike.

Air Vice-Marshal H. Gill, CB, OBE, RAF (Ret'd)

ACKNOWLEDGMENTS

I wish to express my sincere appreciation to the former British Royal Air Force students and the United States Army Air Forces cadets who trained in Terrell, Texas, during World War II. They gave generously of their time to answer my numerous questions. I am also indebted to the former members of the civilian training staff at the Terrell Aviation School who always responded unselfishly to my inquiries.

In England, A. J. "Bert" Allam, Alan Bramson, Paul Ballance, and Don Stebbings provided information. Bert Allam clarified numerous details and provided his unpublished manuscript covering his time in Terrell. Julia Baker copied her late father's Royal Air Force flight log book for me.

In the United States many offered assistance. Among these were former RAF students Eric Gill, Henry Madgwick, Jim Forteith, and Arthur Ridge. Mr. Madgwick, a past mayor of Terrell, allowed access to his large file of official documents, provided his unpublished manuscript, and took time to show me around Terrell and the former auxiliary fields. Eric Gill read an early draft and provided additional comments. Bill Brookover and Ray Flenniken, former flight instructors at the Terrell school, provided information on the aircraft and training syllabus. Rick Brown, a former RAF cadet at No.6 British Flying Training School in Ponca City, Oklahoma, provided historical information assembled by the No.6 BFTS Association. Former Army Air Forces cadets, Ben Brown and L. G. Bue, shared their experiences training with the RAF. Marvin Krieger, Jane Howell, and Pauline Baxter explained the roles of the various civilian instructors at Terrell. Virginia Brewer who, along with her sister Bertha, tended the RAF graves in the Oakland Memorial Cemetery for many years, shared her scrap books, photographs, and clippings.

I am deeply indebted to Dr. Gilbert S. Guinn, professor emeritus in history at Lander University in Greenwood, South Carolina. Dr. Guinn shared his extensive files, including microfilm from the Public Record Office in London and the United States Air Force archives, extensive interview records with former British students, and his unpublished manuscript, and took time to read various drafts, offer suggestions, and answer numerous questions concerning RAF training in the United States.

The staff of the Terrell Public Library, especially Janice Sauer, Katherine Brittain, and Director Rebecca Sullivan, and the staff of the Texas and local history section of the Dallas Public Library provided much assistance. James McCord of the Terrell Heritage Society opened the society's extensive files and answered numerous questions. Ann Kelley, history librarian at the University of Texas at Arlington, located additional information on Major Long and his Dallas-based flight school.

Col. Knox Bishop of the Frontiers of Flight museum, and Joe Norris of the Experimental Aircraft Association provided technical details on World War II flight training. R. D. Nolen spoke to me about his brother Lloyd Nolen, founder of the Confederate Air Force. The Lancaster Texas Wing of the Commemorative Air Force allowed access to the aircraft in their collection.

Jack DeWeese, my good friend, sometimes copilot, sometimes aircraft mechanic, sometimes adventurer, and computer guru, helped with the collection of photographs. His friendship and warped sense of humor are much appreciated.

The majority of this work originally appeared as my master's thesis at the University of Texas at Arlington. I wish to thank my faculty advising committee, Dr. George Green, Dr. Douglas Richmond, and Dr. Gerald Saxon for their help.

The quality of the work is due to these efforts; any errors which remain are mine alone. And finally a word of thanks to my wife Ann who not only provided abundant love and support throughout the effort, but has also shared in my adventures.

The special train thundered southward through the chilly April night in 1942. The train carried Lord Halifax, distinguished, although sometimes controversial, member of the British wartime government, on a somber but vital mission. By the spring of 1942 World War II had raged for more than two and one-half years. In Europe, Austria had been annexed by Germany; Czechoslovakia had been dismembered; Poland, France, Norway, Denmark, and the Low Countries, Belgium, Luxemburg, and Holland, had all fallen. The swift invasion of Russia brought German troops to the outskirts of Moscow and Leningrad. In the first three months of fighting, the Soviets suffered more than two and one-half million casualties.[1]

In the North Atlantic, German U-boats were winning a relentless battle of attrition against Allied merchant shipping essential to British survival. By the end of 1941, German U-boats numbered nearly 250 and construction increased the fleet at a rate of fifteen new submarines per month.[2] By April 1942, more than 5.7 million tons of Allied merchant shipping had been lost in the battle of the Atlantic.[3] These losses far surpassed the capacity of Allied shipyards to construct new ships. In January 1942, U-boats commenced operations off the eastern coast of the United States. Unprotected merchant shipping, especially tankers, silhouetted against the brilliant night lights of cities and coastal areas, became vulnerable targets. In the month before Lord Halifax's mission, thirty merchant ships were lost to German U-boats along the eastern United States.[4] At the end of April 1942, U-507 would be the first U-boat to enter the Gulf of Mexico.[5]

British elation following the entry of the United States into the war four months earlier had been short-lived as setback after setback dogged the Allied cause. The full extent of the United States Navy and Army Air Corps losses at Pearl Harbor were just being realized. Also in the Pacific, Wake Island fell after a heroic defense, the island of Guam had been captured, and the Philippines were poised to fall as Japanese forces prepared for the final assault on the fortress of Corregidor following the surrender of United States and Philippine troops on Bataan.

After being driven from Greece in the Balkans, Crete in the eastern Mediterranean, and Libya in North Africa, British forces now occupied defensive positions deep inside Egypt, before Cairo and the vitally important Suez Canal. In the new Pacific theater, the British navy suffered a crushing defeat only three days after Pearl Harbor when the two mightiest British capital ships in the Pacific, the battleship *Prince of Wales* and the battle cruiser *Repulse* were both sunk by Japanese air attacks off Malaysia in the South China Sea. Two months later, on February 15, 1942, a British army of 130,000 men at Singapore, known as the Gibraltar of the Pacific, surrendered to Japanese forces.

Lord Halifax's April 1942 journey entailed a familiar mission for wartime government officials: to visit British troops in order to maintain morale and to dedicate a new cemetery to those servicemen who had fallen. The only unusual aspect of the journey was the location. The train carrying Lord Halifax had crossed into Texas. His specific destination was the Royal Air Force training facility at Terrell, Texas, officially known as the Number One British Flying Training School, or No.1 BFTS.

---

1. Alan Clark, *Barbarossa; The Russian-German Conflict, 1941-1945* (New York: Morrow, 1965), 145.

2. Winston S. Churchill, *The Second World War: The Hinge of Fate* (Boston: Houghton Mifflin Company, 1950), 109.

3. Compilation from Churchill, *The Hinge of Fate,* 126, and *The Second World*

War: The Grand Alliance (Boston: Houghton Mifflin Company, 1950), 113, 141.

4. Gary Gentile, *Track of the Gray Wolf, U-boat Warfare on the U.S. Eastern Seaboard 1942-1945* (New York: Avon Books, 1989), 268-71.

5. Melanie Wiggins, *Torpedoes in the Gulf, Galveston and the U-boats, 1942-1943* (College Station, Texas: Texas A&M University Press, 1995), 22.

CHAPTER 1

INCEPTION

At the close of World War I in 1918, the Royal Air Force (formerly the Royal Flying Corps) contained 185 squadrons, 291,175 personnel, and was the largest air power in the world. During the 1920s and 1930s Britain's military power declined precipitously. By 1922 the number of squadrons had fallen to twenty-eight, only eight of which were in England, and only three of these were allocated for home defense; the rest of the RAF squadrons were scattered throughout the British Empire. At the same time, the French air force deployed 126 squadrons.[1] Facing financial crisis, successive British governments slashed military spending and appropriations for armaments.

During the 1920s, Marshal of the Royal Air Force Sir Hugh Trenchard, commander of the Royal Flying Corps during World War I, laid the groundwork for the modern RAF. Trenchard fought doggedly and stubbornly in the face of considerable political and inter-service opposition to save the RAF as an independent service. He also formed a reserve of volunteer pilots who trained on weekends and could be called upon in case of emergency. The low cost appealed to the government. These efforts, the establishment of the RAF Technical College at Halton, and the creation of the Royal Air Force college at Cranwell to train a cadre of professional officers earned Trenchard the sobriquet, "father of the RAF" (a term he despised).[2]

In the early 1930s, the Air Council for Research and Development fostered the development of the science of radar and two low-wing, retractable gear, monoplane fighters, the Hawker Hurricane and the Supermarine Spitfire. Both fighters were powered by the new Rolls Royce Merlin engine and mounted the phenomenal armament of eight machine guns. The first Hurricanes began entering service in late 1937, followed by Spitfires in mid-1938.[3] Due to meager funding and limited production facilities, their numbers were pitifully small.

On the eve of World War II, a bare minimum number of Hurricane and Spitfire squadrons, combined with a defensive network made up of early warning radar stations along England's southern coast, anti-aircraft batteries, and an observer corps, all linked by telephone with central command stations, would be ready only just in the nick of time thanks to the dogged determination of a few dedicated RAF officers and a few outspoken public men in the face of abject apathy and political opposition. Historians have laid the blame for Britain's unpreparedness for World War II on the governments of prime ministers Ramsay MacDonald, Stanley Baldwin, and Neville Chamberlain. Only Winston Churchill, out of government and largely discredited, along with a few friends, spoke out warning of the growing threat from Adolf Hitler and Nazism.

But the government's priorities represented the feelings of the vast majority of British citizens whose memories were still fresh of almost a million British Commonwealth dead in Flanders fields during the Great War, the war to end all wars. British citizens and government officials alike branded Churchill a warmonger, scaremonger, and an alarmist. Their faith and the faith of their governments lay first in world organizations such as the League of Nations and treaties to limit armaments, such as the Washington Naval Treaty. When those failed and the massive German rearmament had been confirmed, their fear turned to appeasement. Prominent men such as American aviation hero Col. Charles Lindberg fueled these fears when, after several visits to Germany, he declared in September 1938 that England and France, "are far too weak in the air to protect themselves. . . . a war now might easily result in the loss of European civilization."[4] Chamberlain attempted to calm these fears by meeting personally with Hitler over the matter of the Sudetenland and afterwards wrote, "I got the impression that here was a man who could be relied upon when he had given his word."[5]

After the failure of appeasement in the reoccupation of the
Rhineland, the annexation of Austria, the Sudetenland, and finally
Munich, the German invasion of Poland on September 1, 1939,
forced England and France reluctantly into war. Eight months of
inaction, known as the phony war, followed the fall of Poland until
May 1940 when German panzer and infantry divisions supported
by the Luftwaffe attacked through Belgium into the Low Countries and through the Ardennes into France. Chamberlain resigned
as prime minister and King George VI summoned Winston
Churchill and asked him to form a new national government. Several days later Churchill spoke in the House of Commons:

> I would say to the House, as I have said to those who
> have joined this government: "I have nothing to offer but
> blood, toil, tears, and sweat."
> You ask, what is our policy? I will say: It is to wage war, by
> sea, land and air, with all our might and with all the strength
> God can give us. That is our policy,
> You ask, what is our aim? I can answer in one word; It is
> victory, victory at all costs, victory in spite of all terror, vic-
> tory however long and hard the road may be; for without
> victory, there can be no survival.[6]

Although the necessary aircraft types were starting to be produced
in greater numbers, the pilots and aircrews to man them were an
entirely different matter.

Even before the beginning of World War II, British Royal Air
Force officials recognized the need for training aircrew in Commonwealth countries in the event of war. Drawbacks to flight training in Britain during wartime included the abysmal English weather,
the limited size of the country, and the very real possibility of enemy attack.

Initial discussions with Commonwealth governments before the
war produced mixed results. Southern Rhodesia, Australia, and
New Zealand responded quickly and favorably. Other Common-

wealth governments were agreeable. The political climate in South Africa, however, precluded negotiations with that country. In Canada, the premier, W. L. Mackenzie King, stubbornly refused to consider RAF flight training.[7]

The outbreak of hostilities resulted in the implementation of the Empire Air Training Scheme (later renamed the British Commonwealth Air Training Plan) and both Canada and South Africa pledged their full cooperation. Under this plan British pilots and aircrews were trained in a number of Commonwealth countries including Canada, Australia, India, New Zealand, Kenya, Southern Rhodesia, and South Africa. The first courses in the new schools in Canada, Australia, and New Zealand began training in April 1940.[8]

British flight students in the Empire Air Training Scheme encountered conditions as diverse as grass hut barracks and blazing summer heat in Southern Rhodesia, airfield elevations more than 6,000 feet above sea level, along with a confused and often hostile political climate in South Africa, and harsh Canadian winters. Even Britain's primary trainer, the beloved de Havilland Tiger Moth, suffered from the intense heat, high humidity, and the extreme elevations of some overseas training areas due to its small four cylinder engine and wooden, fabric-covered, wings. Tiger Moths had to be withdrawn from several of these areas, but the American trainers that replaced them often fared little better.[9]

As the Empire Air Training Scheme began to take shape, it became obvious that additional aircrew training facilities would be required. British officials naturally looked to the United States for possible assistance. Early conversations in the spring of 1940 between Lord Halifax, then British secretary of state for foreign affairs, and Joseph Kennedy, the United States ambassador to Britain, concerning the possibility of training Royal Air Force pilots in the United States proved encouraging.

Later conversations, however, between Lord Lothian, the British ambassador to the United States, and Under-Secretary of State Sumner Welles were not so positive. Several factors concerned

Welles, including United States neutrality, the strong isolationist feeling in the country, the possible effect on President Franklin Roosevelt's reelection campaign for an unprecedented third term, the large number of United States citizens of German and Italian descent possibly sympathetic to the Axis cause, and a large population of Irish-Americans who harbored no love for Great Britain. In June 1940, after conferring with President Roosevelt, Welles denied the British request.[10]

There also existed considerable doubt that the necessary military facilities and equipment could be made available due to the United States' own extensive rearmament program. In particular, there existed a shortage of advanced training aircraft in the United States. While several types of civilian light aircraft such as Pipers, Taylorcrafts, and Aeroncas could theoretically be used for the initial phase of flight training, known as primary, advanced trainers that offered the performance and sophisticated systems of operational aircraft were in short supply.[11]

Despite the official rejection of the British request for training facilities, conversations at various levels and on both sides of the Atlantic continued. In an August 28, 1940, meeting in London, Army Air Corps Col. Carl Spaatz told the British air member for training that the army could not spare the facilities or equipment for British training. Spaatz did, however, suggest the possibility of utilizing civilian facilities and specifically recommended the favorable training conditions in Oklahoma and Texas.[12]

On the same day in New York, Henry Morgenthau, U.S. treasury secretary, who had been entrusted by President Roosevelt with coordinating aid to Britain, met with British Under-Secretary of State Capt. H. H. Balfour and also discussed training in civilian facilities. Balfour later cabled the air ministry, "The President of the United States is well disposed toward such a scheme and would take a personal interest in it."[13]

Both Morgenthau and Colonel Spaatz stated that for such a plan to be politically acceptable, and to avoid the necessity for congressional approval, British students would have to enter the United

States in civilian clothes through Canada, and training would exclude any live gunnery or bombing practice. Even though these discussions were encouraging, the shortage of training aircraft remained a major problem. Morgenthau hinted that President Roosevelt, as commander in chief, might consider diverting the necessary aircraft from U.S. production schedules, but made no commitment.[14]

Following these discussions, plans to train British pilots in the United States gained momentum in the fall of 1940 after the re-election of President Roosevelt to a third term. Roosevelt actively sought to assist Great Britain short of war and four days before the election stated, "Our policy is to give all possible material aid to the nations which still resist aggression."[15] From this desire to aid Britain, emerged the concept of lend-lease. Until this time, the British government, through a purchasing commission located in the United States, placed all orders for war materiel directly with American companies and paid for the equipment and supplies in cash.[16] Under lend-lease, materiel would be purchased by the United States and "loaned" to the British under a central allocation system managed by the United States government. Winston Churchill described the lend-lease bill approved by Congress and signed by President Roosevelt on March 11, 1941, as "The most unsordid act in the history of any nation."[17] The Lend-Lease Act paved the way for training British pilots and aircrew in the United States.

Against this background, Air Commodore George Pirie, the air attaché and member of the British purchasing commission in Washington, D.C., received a phone call on March 5 from Maj. Gen. Henry H. Arnold, the United States Army assistant chief of staff and Army Air Corps chief.[18] When Pirie arrived in Arnold's office, he found fifteen others present. "I think you know all of these people," Arnold said with a wave of his hand and then without waiting for an answer, "You've been worrying me for a year and a half about training, now let's talk." Arnold continued, "As soon as the Lend-Lease Bill is through we are going to offer you up to 260

Stearmans and Fairchilds and up to 285 Harvards or Yales on loan for training purposes. I understand these aircraft are to be used in this country: and here are six of our best civilian school operators who are prepared to co-operate with you on this scheme."[19] Pirie cabled the air ministry in London the following day with the encouraging news of his meeting with Arnold, and added more details in a letter to the air ministry the following week.

Several meetings followed this initial discussion and General Arnold traveled to England in April 1941 to meet with British officials and senior RAF officers to discuss aid requirements and to get a firsthand view of British operations. While in England, Arnold met with Air Chief Marshal Sir Charles Portal and Air Vice Marshal A. G. R. Garrod, British air member for training. Arnold and Garrod discussed the proposed training of British pilots in the United States, the additional prospect of training British navigators, and the possibility of American pilots ferrying British aircraft purchased in the United States across the Atlantic.[20]

From these meetings, and later meetings with the United States Navy, four distinctly different programs to train British aircrew in the United States emerged. Two of the programs incorporated RAF students directly into the established United States Army Air Corps and Navy flight training programs. These two plans were known as the Arnold Scheme, named after General Arnold, and the Towers Scheme, named after Navy Vice Admiral John H. Towers.[21] Another, although lesser known, program trained British navigators at the Pan American Airways navigation school in Coral Gables, Florida.

The other program, known as the British Flying Training Schools, utilized civilian flight schools that already had experience training Army Air Corps pilots. The British Flying Training Schools provided students with flight training from primary through advanced at the same location (the British often referred to these schools as the All Through Training Scheme). This innovation, unique among the various training schemes, offered faster training and greater efficiency. The civilian flight schools provided the facilities, and the United States Army provided the necessary aircraft and support. The British considered the cost, $21.60 per hour for primary flight training and $32.70 per hour for advanced flight training (which included basic training) to be high, but agreed to the plan.[22] Even though much of the cost of the program would be provided under lend-lease, the British government agreed to fund sixty percent of the initial cost of the new schools in order to avoid delay. These amounts, plus interest, would be repaid over several years by the school operators. RAF officials optimistically projected that British students could begin training by the end of May 1941.

Six civilian flight schools dedicated to RAF pilot training were initially constructed in the United States. A seventh school, located in Sweetwater, Texas, opened later, but operated only briefly from June to August 1942.[23]

School	Location
No.1	Terrell, Texas
No.2	Lancaster, California
No.3	Miami, Oklahoma
No.4	Mesa, Arizona
No.5	Clewiston, Florida
No.6	Ponca City, Oklahoma

The army recommended Maj. William F. Long of Dallas, Texas, to be one of the civilian flight school operators in the new program. His school would be designated No.1 British Flying Training School.

Born on a Missouri farm on October 19, 1894, William Long dreamed of becoming a flyer almost as soon as he could ride a horse. Long left his parents' farm in 1917 and traveled to Texas to learn to fly. Trained in San Antonio by the famous Eddie Stinson, Long joined the army shortly after the United States' entry into World War I. Long's lifetime vocation began to take shape during advanced flying training in France. Of the forty-five pilots with Long in the 24th Aero Squadron, twenty-eight were killed in training accidents, while only four were killed in combat.[24]

After the war, Long, mustered out of the service in 1920, returned to San Antonio and opened his own flight school with a surplus Curtiss JN-4D Jenny as a trainer.[25] From his personal experiences, Long believed that teaching someone to fly could not be rushed and he worked to develop one of the first educational approaches to flight training. Students, however, were not plentiful.

To make ends meet, Long frequently left the school in the hands of his assistant instructor and took other jobs, including selling surplus aircraft throughout the United States, Mexico, and Central America. From contacts developed in Mexico, Long secured contracts to fly mail for the Mexican government and payrolls for Mexican companies doing business in remote parts of Mexico. At one point he tried to interest United States government officials in an airmail contract between Dallas and the Mexican border. This idea met with no encouragement. In fact, years later Long remarked, "They told me if I valued my neck, I should go back to the farm."[26]

In 1926 Long gave his airfield to the city of San Antonio and moved all of his flight operations to Love Field, a little-used grass field six miles northwest of Dallas, Texas, built in 1917 to train army pilots for World War I.[27] By selling airplanes (and often giving flying lessons free with the purchase), instructing, and taking other jobs such as barnstorming for a summer with the Wendel brothers (who later became famous for their racing planes), Long slowly improved his business.

In 1932 C. E. Harmon became Long's partner and general manager of the school, now known as Dallas Aviation School and Air College. Long had never given up the idea of an airmail contract and an airline. In the 1930s airlines could not make a profit by transporting passengers alone; only with a government airmail contract could an airline remain in business. In 1934 Long received an airmail contract, designated AM15, between Amarillo, Texas, and Brownsville, Texas. The resulting airline, named Long and Harmon Air Lines, flying Ford Tri-motors, operated profitably for the first year, then T. E. Braniff, owner and president of Braniff Airways, purchased the airline.[28]

In a January 12, 1939, address to Congress, President Roosevelt called for a massive rearmament campaign including increased expenditures for aircraft procurement and expansion of the Army Air Corps.[29] The previous year the army had graduated only 300 pilots from its only training facility at Randolph Field in San Antonio, Texas, and the proposed expansion program far surpassed the capabilities of the army training command.[30] Against considerable internal resistance General Arnold decided to enlist civilian flight schools in the expanded army pilot training effort.[31]

By 1939 Long was an established and respected flying school operator. Due to his reputation and continued dedication to flight training as an educational process, the army awarded Long one of the first civilian contracts to train Army Air Corps pilots.[32] The first class arrived at Love Field in July 1939.[33] Training continued for eighteen months until it became obvious the facilities at Love Field were no longer adequate for the level of activity required by the army contract. By 1940 the city of Dallas had constructed three hard surface runways and a modern terminal building at Love Field, and the Civil Aeronautics Authority (the CAA, predecessor of the Federal Aviation Administration) had installed a radio-equipped control tower. Several flight schools and three airlines, American, Braniff, and Delta, used the field.

Long constructed another primary school in Brady, Texas, located 180 miles southwest of Dallas. Army cadets began training at the new facility in March 1941. Long also trained Army Air Corps pilots at Hicks Field, twelve miles northwest of Fort Worth, and received one of the first civilian contracts to train aircraft mechanics for the army.[34]

In view of Long's training credentials and successful history with the United States Army Air Corps, it was only natural for the army to recommend Long to the British commission charged with implementing the training of British pilots in the United States. Impressed with Long's attitude, accomplishments, and facilities, the British commission readily agreed with the recommendation. By the late spring of 1941 the various details had been worked out and only the selection of a new training site remained.[35]

A group of businessmen from Terrell, Texas, located thirty-five miles east of Dallas, led by Chamber of Commerce president Angus Dickson, had earlier called on Long in his Love Field office. The members of the group were interested in promoting aviation and a new airport in Terrell. Later the group enlisted the aid of Sam Rayburn, Speaker of the United States House of Representatives, who contacted Long on behalf of Terrell. Long had also been contacted by Charles Williams, the local Gulf Oil distributor, and Buck Rowe, Gulf Oil's aviation director. Both men touted Terrell as an airport site.[36]

Terrell at first glance seems an unlikely location for a wartime flight training facility. The city's namesake, Robert Terrell, born in Murfreesboro, Tennessee, on February 20, 1820, came to Texas in 1840. An educated man with an engaging personality, Terrell soon found many friends in the new land, including Sam Houston, president of the Republic of Texas. As a professional surveyor, Terrell's talents were in demand and Houston appointed him a surveyor of the public domain.

In 1854 Terrell surveyed the boundaries of the newly created Kaufman County and also surveyed many of the early land sales in the county. The initial county survey included locating the geographic center of the county for a possible county seat site. Of the several county seat sites proposed, the one surveyed by Terrell was selected and became the town of Kaufman in 1854. Terrell later settled on a farm ten miles north of Kaufman on land received for his services. Except for service in the Confederate Army during the Civil War, where he rose to the rank of major, Terrell remained a farmer until his death in 1881.

In 1873 the Texas and Pacific Railroad completed an extension west from Longview in East Texas to the north central Texas community of Dallas. The line passed through the northern portion of Kaufman County near Terrell's farm. Two enterprising developers, C. C. Nash and John Moore, purchased 320 acres of land for five dollars an acre along the railroad right of way and donated eighty-seven acres to the railroad for a townsite with the stipulation that a depot would be located in the town. Merchants and other adventurers drawn by the railroad soon arrived at the stop. The new town acquired a wide-open reputation and became noted for its saloons, gambling halls, and high stakes games of chance. Two names were proposed for the town: Terrell and Moore. At a citywide election, local citizens selected Terrell as the name of the town, while the main streets were named Moore and Nash.[37]

Located in a rich agricultural area, Terrell was recognized by other developers for its potential. After only eighteen months the new town had grown to a population of 1,800. By 1900 Terrell had 6,300 inhabitants; two railroads served the town, and churches and schools had replaced the saloons and gambling halls, while residential areas rich in Gothic architecture circled the town. Work began in 1912 to pave the city's dirt streets, which had habitually turned into quagmires of mud with each rain.[38]

In 1923 the new Interurban Electric Railway linked Terrell and Dallas with sixteen express runs per day. The Interurban reduced the travel time from Terrell to Dallas to one hour and twenty minutes and included twenty-one stops along the way. With expanded all-weather highways and the growing popularity of personal automobiles, the Interurban discontinued the Dallas to Terrell line in 1932.[39]

By 1940, Terrell had grown into a progressive and prosperous town of 10,480 inhabitants. Sturdy two- and three-story brick buildings containing several banks, two theaters, a hotel, cafés, and various assorted retail, clothing, and drugstores lined Moore Avenue. On the outskirts of town were cotton gins, farm implements dealers, feed stores, and new car dealerships. The main street now formed part of the new national highway system as US 80, which extended from Columbus, Georgia, to the west coast. The town lay peacefully between two worlds, the old agricultural age which had existed from the late nineteenth century through the Great Depression, and the new age of modern warfare about to dawn.

The inception of the Terrell airport, known officially as the Kaufman County Airport during World War II, and the RAF training facility can be traced back to the formation of the Terrell flying club and an air show staged by the flying club in December 1940. Local citizens formed the flying club, sponsored by the Terrell Junior Chamber of Commerce, in the fall of 1940. The club originally consisted of one instructor, Doug Pettit, and approximately twenty members, who paid one dollar per month in dues. Pettit's two Piper Cubs, one powered by a fifty horsepower engine and the other by a forty horsepower engine, were used for flight training. Later, a Taylorcraft replaced one of the Cubs. The club elected Dr. L. W. Johnson to be club president and a local resident, R. B. Mosley, donated a small portable building for the club's use.[40]

For its flying activities, the club leased a field just south of town for five dollars per month.[41] Within several months a telephone and a small hangar were added to the field. The field gained brief notoriety in February 1941 when an Army Boeing P-12 fighter became lost on a flight from Chanute Field, Illinois, to Dallas Love Field and landed on the club's field.[42]

The impromptu air show presented by the club in December 1940 proved to be a tremendous success with Terrell citizens and generated increased interest in aviation and in establishing a local airport. The air show, described as a "financial dud," featured aerobatics and several aircraft fly-bys. The hit of the show turned out to be a clown hired to perform several skits. The clown's first act, a delayed parachute drop, came off successfully, but only after the clown borrowed a parachute from one of the pilots. The clown next stepped off the running board of a speeding car and was knocked unconscious. After he came to, the clown then rode on the front of a car as it crashed through a flaming board wall and was again rendered unconscious. An observer noted, "As a matter of fact, he was unconscious most of the afternoon, but the crowd loved it."[43]

An airport had been advocated by Terrell citizens before December 1940, but the air show added impetus to the efforts. This interest led to several discussions among leading Terrell businessmen, the Chamber of Commerce, and the Civil Aeronautics Authority. CAA officials inspected the most often mentioned airport site, which lay midway between Terrell and Kaufman, but these plans never materialized.[44] During this period, a delegation of business leaders from Terrell met with Major Long in Dallas, as well as with other potential operators, including the owner of another private flight school interested in a site to train Army Air Corps pilots. Inquiries were also made to the Works Progress Administration (WPA) concerning possible federal funds for an airport in Terrell.[45] These discussions and inquiries produced no results; but interest in establishing an airport remained high.

In the late spring of 1941, the delegation from Terrell again met with Major Long to discuss the possibility of establishing a training facility in Terrell. By this time Long had concluded his negotiations with British officials. Although impressed by the Terrell citizens' presentation and enthusiasm, Long had one primary concern—time was critical.

Toward the end of May 1941, Long, along with his operations manager L. H. Luckey and RAF Squadron Leader Stuart Mills, visited Terrell. They inspected the field used by the flying club, located one mile south of town. The 526 acres, much of it still planted in cotton, located on two farms owned by Joel R. Bond and C. K. Patton, required minor grading and drainage work, the relocation of a high-voltage electrical power line which ran across the northwest corner of the field, and the removal of trees and several small houses.

Kaufman County Judge Monroe Ashworth assured Long that the county could issue general warrants to purchase the land and avoid unnecessary delay. The land would be leased to Long for one dollar per year and the city of Terrell would extend water, sewer, and electrical lines to the site, and provide free utilities (except gas) for ten years. The city owned the municipal water works and the local electric company. In return, Long agreed to construct improvements estimated to cost $265,000. Pleased with the site, Squadron Leader Mills commented, "I only hope that your extraordinary brand of Texas hospitality won't overcome our boys."[46]

After Long and the city reached a tentative agreement, the May 30, 1941, *Terrell Daily Tribune* banner headline proclaimed "RAF TO BASE HERE" and underneath in smaller but still formidable letters, "300 Future British Flyers Coming." Even though the announcement met with almost unanimous excitement and approval, one young woman in Terrell, Bertha Brewer, thought after reading the news, "Oh my goodness! Foreigners in Terrell?"[47]

Soon after the announcement, Kaufman County commissioners realized that general warrants could not be used to purchase property and the statutes dictated a countywide bond election. Bond elections required notices and public hearings, which would considerably delay and possibly void the agreement.

At an emergency meeting held on the evening of June 10 at the Terrell city hall, Walter P. Allen, president of the American National Bank of Terrell, personally pledged $2,500 and another $5,000 from the bank to purchase the land, pending approval of the bond issue. Leland Marshal quickly pledged $1,000, Dr. W. F. Alexander pledged $500, and Chester and Walter Stallings pledged $250. Other enthusiastic citizens joined in with pledges ranging from $100 to $1,000. Pledges that evening totaled $22,000 toward the $35,000 purchase price of the land. Additional pledges received during the next two days secured the remaining amount.[48]

Long and city officials signed the agreement on Flag Day, June 14, 1941, which many citizens considered symbolic. Long immediately authorized John Pirtle, the general contractor who had just completed the Brady, Texas, Army Air Corps training facility for Long, to come to Terrell and begin work. Local engineer J. K. LaRoe produced contour maps of the site for the grading and leveling portion of the work.[49]

Even though the worst effects of the Great Depression had begun to subside by 1941, more than 100 men showed up for work by six o'clock in the morning on the day the contractor arrived in Terrell. Forty men were hired immediately, and as more materials arrived at the site, the construction force grew to 150 men.[50]

Long appointed Luckey to direct the Terrell operation. Long had first met Luckey in Venita, Oklahoma, in the early 1920s, when Luckey traded a Packard automobile to Long for an airplane. Luckey later assisted Long in dealing with the Curtiss Aeroplane and Engine Company (Long sold surplus Curtiss airplanes), then joined Long in the new airline, Long and Harmon Air Lines. When T. E. Braniff purchased the airline in 1935, Luckey remained with Braniff Airways and became its operations manager. Luckey left Braniff in 1941 to rejoin Long as the director of the Terrell school.[51] Incorporated as a separate entity, the Terrell RAF facility became the Terrell Aviation School.

1. Peter Townsend, *Duel of Eagles* (New York: Simon and Schuster, 1971), 47.

2. Trevor N. Dupuy, Curt Johnson, and David L. Bongard, *The Harper Encyclopedia of Military Biography* (New York: Harper Collins, 1992), 752.

3. William Green, *Famous Fighters of the Second World War* (New York: Hanover House, 1958), 20, 26.

4. William Manchester, *The Last Lion: Winston Spencer Churchill, Alone 1932-1940* (Boston: Little, Brown and Company, 1988), 316.

5. Ibid., 339.

6. Ibid., 682-83.

7. Townsend, 137.

8. Denis Richards, *Royal Air Force 1939-1945, Vol. I, The Fight at Odds* (London: Her Majesty's Stationery Office, 1953), 74.

9. American Fairchild PT-19s, which replaced some of the British Tiger Moths, had larger six-cylinder Ranger engines of 175 or 200 horsepower, but their plywood-covered wooden wings and wooden center sections exhibited many of the same problems encountered by the Tiger Moths.

10. Gilbert S. Guinn, "British Aircrew Training in the United States 1941-1945," *Air Power History* (Summer 1995): 9.

11. While the military did not use the light civilian planes for training, the Civilian Pilot Training program (CPT) taught many young men destined for military flight training the essentials of flight in these planes. For a good description of a future Marine Corps pilot in the CPT program in Denton, Texas, see: Samuel Hynes, *Flights of Passage* (New York: Simon and Schuster Inc., 1988), 14-19.

12. "Development of Training Facilities in U.S.A." memorandum by A.M.T. located AIR 20/1387, Public Record Office, London.

13. A.C. 39(40) "Air Council: Training of Pilots in the United States of America," memorandum by A.M.T. 10 September 1940, located in AIR 20/1387, Public Record Office, London.

14. Ibid.

15. Winston S. Churchill, *The Second World War: Their Finest Hour* (Boston: Houghton Mifflin Company, 1949), 553.

16. On November 4, 1939, President Roosevelt signed a revision to the neutrality law which allowed Britain and France to buy weapons on a "cash and carry" basis.

17. Churchill, *Their Finest Hour*, 569.

18. Nicknamed "Hap" early in his career because he was always happy, Arnold graduated from West Point in 1908 and later joined the aviation branch of the Signal Corps where he learned to fly from the Wright brothers in 1911. Thomas M. Coffey, *Hap: the Story of the U.S. Air Force and the Man Who Built It, General Henry H. "Hap" Arnold* (New York: The Viking Press, 1982), 40-45.

19. Letter dated 13 March 1941 from George Pirie to Air Marshal A. G. R. Garrod, Director of Equipment, Air Ministry London, located in AIR 20/1387. Also, Air 32/14 *History of Flying Training* (London: Public Record Office), 468-75.

20. Arnold planned a low-key trip, but the British gave him VIP treatment. After meeting with high ranking military officers and government officials, Arnold had dinner with Winston Churchill and his wife, then stayed up all night discussing the war with Churchill. Toward the end of his trip the British arranged an audience with King George VI. H. H. Arnold, *Global Mission* (New York: Harper and Brothers, 1949), 215-38.

21. Towers became Naval Aviator No. 3 after being taught to fly by the legendary Glenn Curtiss. Clark G. Reynolds, *Admiral John H. Towers: The Struggle for Naval Air Supremacy* (Annapolis, Maryland: Naval Institute Press, 1991), 31-35.

22. Letter dated March 31, 1941, from Air Commodore G. C. Pirie to Major E. H. Alexander, Office of the Chief of the Army Air Corps. "History of the Dallas Aviation School, Love Field, Dallas, Texas, 1 July 1939 - 15 March 1941." Located in the United States Air Force Historical Research Agency archives at Maxwell Air Force Base, Alabama, hereafter referred to as Maxwell.

23. Guinn, "British Aircrew Training," 12.

24. *Terrell Daily Tribune*, August 26, 1941.

25. Ibid. Long left the army with the rank of captain but remained in the reserves and was later promoted to major. Contemporary publications and letters almost always refer to Long by his military rank.

26. Ibid.

27. In a March 2, 1969, *Dallas Morning News* article, Long said he bought an unused hangar at Love Field in order to get eight disassembled and crated Curtiss JN-4Ds stored in the hangar.

28. *Dallas Morning News*, August 21, 1976. The purchase of Long and Harmon Air Lines expanded Braniff's route system from Chicago on the Great Lakes to the Mexican border.

29. Wesley Frank Craven and James Lea Cate, Eds. *The Army Air Forces in World War II, Vol. I, Plans and Early Operations January 1939 to August 1942* (Chicago: University of Chicago Press, 1948), 104.

30. Ibid., 111. Several years later the army graduated 50,000 pilots in one year, and in 1944, 105,000 pilots graduated. Arnold, *Global Mission*, 530.

31. One of Arnold's staff officers, Lt. Col. Ira Eaker, summed up the staff's feelings when he argued that the new policy would be "just plain murder." Coffey, 196.

32. General Arnold met with Long and seven other flight school operators to get their help in starting the new program. Asked about funds for new facilities, Arnold replied, "you can borrow the money, can't you, until I can get congressional appropriations?" With no more than Arnold's promise to try and pay them, the operators agreed to the new plan. Arnold, *Global Mission*, 181.

33. Long's initial contract, W535 ac-12872, called for 65 hours of primary flight instruction and 225 hours of ground instruction in a twelve-week course. The army later amended the course (contract W535 ac-15369) to 60 hours of flight instruction and 140 hours of ground school in a ten-week course. "History of the Dallas Aviation School, Love Field, Dallas, Texas, 1 July 1939-15 March 1941," Maxwell, microfilm roll A2281. Also, Schirmer, "AAC & AAF Civil Primary Flying Schools 1939-1945: Part VII Dallas Primary," 216, 218.

34. *Terrell Daily Tribune*, August 26, 1941. During World War I, Royal Canadian Air Force pilots trained at Hicks Field, then known as Taliaferro Field.

35. In a meeting with British officials, Long reportedly told Capt. Harold Balfour, under-secretary of state for air, not to worry about the expense; he would take British prized Hereford bulls for breeding stock on his Texas ranch as partial payment since, "they're going to be bombed to hell anyway." According to the story, the British agreed, but the plan fell through due to wartime restrictions on transporting cattle. Willard Wiener, *Two Hundred Thousand Flyers, the Story of the Civilian-AAF Pilot Training Program* (Washington: The Infantry Journal, 1945), 43-44.

36. *Terrell Daily Tribune*, August 26, 1941.

37. Jack Stoltz, *Terrell Texas 1873-1973: From Open Country to Modern City* (San Antonio: The Naylor Company, 1973), 14.

38. Ibid., 115.

39. Ibid., 124-26.

40. *Terrell Daily Tribune*, January 18, 1941.

41. Ibid., January 11, 1941.

42. Ibid., February 19, 1941.

43. Ibid., August 26, 1941.

44. Ibid., January 10, 1941, February 6, 1941, February 13, 1941, March 28, 1941

45. Ibid., March 26, 1941

46. Ibid., May 30, 1941.

47. Quoted on page 82 of a collection of undated essays arranged by the Terrell Heritage Society titled *Terrell Centennial 1873-1973*, located in the Terrell Public Library. Other sources have attributed virtually the same quote to Bertha's sister Virginia.

48. *Terrell Daily Tribune*, June 11, 1941.

49. Ibid., June 19, 1941.

50. Ibid., July 1, 1941 and July 7, 1941.

51. Ibid., August 26, 1941.

Royal Air Force officials had been overly optimistic in anticipating that flight training in the new BFTS program could begin by the end of May 1941. Delays in congressional approval of lend-lease appropriations, further delays in negotiations with the civilian contractors, and the site selection process all prolonged implementation of the program. The complex program, however, had already been activated in England before the delays became apparent.

The BFTS training program anticipated that each school would house 200 students consisting of four courses of fifty cadets each. Courses were scheduled to last twenty weeks, ten weeks of primary, five weeks of basic, and five weeks of advanced flight training. A new course was scheduled to arrive in Terrell every five weeks to begin training.

Two RAF officers were assigned to each school. The RAF selected Wing Commander F. W. Hilton, a bomber pilot with considerable combat experience, as the Terrell commanding officer and chief flying instructor (CFI), and Squadron Leader A. Beveridge as the chief ground instructor (CGI). Before leaving for the United States, both officers were extensively briefed by air ministry officers. Officials told Hilton and Beveridge that the civilian flight school operators selected for the new program were extremely sensitive regarding their authority and course curriculum. The RAF officers assigned to the schools would act only in an advisory capacity and in no way attempt to alter the established school flight training program.[1] In addition, the officers were warned that isolationist feelings in the United States were strongest in western states such as Texas. The officers were instructed in the strongest terms to avoid any discussion of the war, or the possible entry of the United States into the war, for fear of creating adverse publicity that might offend local citizens.[2] Due to the novelty of the program, Hilton and Beveridge found that there were no manuals, ground school supplies, or other training publications available from the air ministry. Frustrated, Hilton and Beveridge returned to their previous commands at No.11 Elementary Flying Training School (EFTS) located at Perth and operational training units (OTU) at Heston and Upper Heyford and gathered manuals, publications, and ground school supplies.[3]

After arriving in the United States, Hilton and Beveridge conferred with the RAF Delegation in Washington, D.C., headed by Group Capt. D. V. Carnegie, an early and enthusiastic supporter of the new training program. Besides discussing training matters, Carnegie reiterated the warnings expressed earlier by the air ministry. After the briefing Hilton and Beveridge must have approached their new assignment with some apprehension as they traveled to Texas in late May 1941.[4]

Once Hilton and Beveridge arrived in Dallas they quickly discovered that virtually everything they had been told by the air ministry in Britain and the RAF Delegation in Washington had been incorrect. The Terrell Aviation School staff consisted of Luckey as director, chief advanced flight instructor E. Van Lloyd, a former airline pilot and Army Air Corps instructor, chief primary flight instructor R. D. Griffin, chief ground school instructor I. V. French, and maintenance supervisor J. Hayden. The staff proved to be not only experienced and cooperative, but eager to incorporate RAF training methods into the school curriculum. The staff especially wanted to build a strong school spirit since this would be the first BFTS.[5]

Hilton and Beveridge were also surprised to find an abundance of pro-British sentiment in North Texas. Many local residents who greeted the RAF officers openly expressed the opinion that the United States should not only join Britain in the war, but the sooner the United States entered the war, the better. The month before, the *Terrell Daily Tribune* commented, "In cafes, department stores along Moore Avenue and in private homes the average Terrell citizen thinks it will be only a matter of months or weeks until the United States becomes involved in the war which is now raging in most parts of the world."[6]

It quickly became apparent that the primary obstacle confronting the establishment of an RAF training facility would be the age-old bane of military organizations, logistics. The two officers found an almost total absence of aircraft, parachutes, equipment, supplies, and support facilities for the new school.[7] Not only had equipment not arrived, but apparently no system had been implemented for procuring equipment and supplies.

The U.S. Army Materiel Division at Wright Field in Dayton, Ohio, issued a memorandum a week later on June 6, 1941, authorizing area supply centers, including Randolph Field in San Antonio, Texas, the depot responsible for supporting the Terrell operation, to supply equipment to the RAF schools. This memorandum provided that "The use of Air Corps equipment and supplies, airplanes, engines, parachutes, spare parts, gasoline, oil, etc. required for the operation of these schools is authorized under Lend-Lease procedures. All equipment and supplies with the exception of food and medicine will be provided by the Air Corps thru normal supply channels."[8] But implementation of this directive at the local level took time. While Luckey attempted to deal with the army supply system, the two RAF officers worked to develop an effective training schedule and syllabus.

The cadets of Course 1 had been selected in Britain specifically for the new program. Under normal RAF procedures, cadets selected for flight training were sent to two weeks training in a Reception Wing to receive uniforms (kit), inoculations, and "a general introduction to service life."[9] From the Reception Wing, cadets passed to an Initial Training Wing (ITW) for eight weeks of instruction in mathematics, air navigation, meteorology, drill, physical training, and general studies before going on to flight training. After ITW, cadets destined for flight school were given the rank of leading aircraftman, abbreviated LAC.

The first cadets bound for the new American program were selected from ITW units and sent across the stormy North Atlantic in converted merchant ships to Canada. Aboard the ships, cadets were packed into damp, occasionally lice-infested, former cargo holds, sleeping in hastily erected multi-tier bunks or hammocks, and subjected to the constant dread of a torpedo attack by German U-boats and seasickness. In the rough seas, numerous buckets for the relief of seasickness were placed on the rolling decks and once filled, inevitably overturned.

Many cadets traveled to Canada on the ex-French liner *Pasteur* built in 1939 and taken over by the British after the fall of France.[10] Later in the war cadets crossed the Atlantic in converted ocean liners such as the *Queen Mary* and *Queen Elizabeth*, which offered improved conditions, but were still crowded and uncomfortable. On many of these later crossings, German and Italian prisoners of war captured in North Africa shared the converted liners with British students destined for the United States. Many of the British cadets felt that, overall, the prisoners of war were better treated than the cadets during the Atlantic crossing.[11]

British students landed at Halifax, Nova Scotia, and then traveled by train to a dispatching station, located initially in Toronto, Ontario, and later in Moncton, New Brunswick. Early travel arrangements, as well as facilities at the dispatching stations were crude. Jim Forteith, later to join Course 9 in Terrell, and a draft of one hundred students arrived around midnight in Moncton after a train ride across the desolate Canadian landscape from Halifax. No provision had been made for food on the trip and the cadets arrived sore, filthy, and hungry. They also arrived after the mess hall had closed. A very proper RAF group captain met the students for an introductory talk only to be greeted by a chorus of "No talk, just food, food."[12] The officer wisely opened the kitchen, where the students ate ravenously, and then the officer set up a delousing station. The RAF steadily improved the Moncton facilities, and in time the dispatching station became a model of efficiency.

Once in Canada, the first students bound for schools in the United States faced a situation unlike any other in the RAF. To maintain at least the appearance of American neutrality, U.S. officials had specified that British flight students would enter the country in civilian clothes. In accordance with this agreement, cadets in Canada were issued a grey flannel suit and two pairs of pants to wear while in the United States and applied for a U.S. visa in order to enter the country. Some contemporary news stories reported that British civilians were to undergo flight training in the United States.[13] Later sources have reported that the cadets were officially released from the RAF in Canada and entered the United States as civilians; then at the end of training they traveled back to Canada and were recalled to duty in the RAF. Even though this story has been repeated, the cadets were never in any doubt that they remained in the RAF while training in the United States.

The Canadian dispatching station stored the cadet's kit (except a uniform to be worn on base), gas mask, and steel helmet. The real concern had to do with the great distance from any established RAF facility or command structure during this detached training period. Under this rather unusual arrangement, cadets were instructed to address all problems to the director of the civilian flight school and, "Since the airmen will not be subject to Air Force discipline when at the training center, and as a consequence they must be placed on their honor to conform strictly with the school regulations, and outside the school to speak with discretion and conduct themselves with propriety."[14]

Apparently the RAF supply system in Canada also suffered from the same confusion regarding the new program as the Army Air Corps supply system in the United States. The first cadets, unaware of their ultimate destination, received an initial issue of thick woolen socks, woolen underwear, a heavy long sleeve shirt, and a small clothing allowance to cover additional civilian items. Cadets were strongly advised to spend this allowance on a heavy overcoat. Most cadets followed this advice and arrived in the Texas summer heat outfitted with woolen underwear and an overcoat.[15]

The train journey from Toronto or Moncton to Terrell presented the young British students with an ever changing landscape full of new sights and experiences. Depending on the dispatching station, students traveled through Detroit or Chicago, and then south to Saint Louis. Layovers in these cities provided a chance to explore, and the cadets took advantage of the stops to visit local sights and sample fresh and exotic foods. Most of these young men had never been far from home and as they traveled ever southward they were awed by the vast expanse of the United States.[16] As the train neared Texas and its final destination, thoughts turned more and more to the prospect of flight training and its unknowns.

Due to the overly optimistic implementation of the new flight training program in Britain, the first contingent of fifty cadets arrived in Dallas on June 2, 1941.[17] The cadets arrived before the final agreement between Long and the city of Terrell had been signed, before aircraft or equipment had arrived, and before construction of the Terrell school had even started. The first cadets were housed in the Dallas Aviation School facilities at Love Field, now largely vacant (except for the army mechanics class) since the completion of the new Brady, Texas, location.

The other schools in the BFTS program experienced similar problems. No.2 BFTS in Lancaster, California, and No.4 BFTS in Mesa, Arizona, opened about the same time as the Dallas school (although the first site selected for the Mesa school had to be rejected when it was found to be on Indian land). The first students for No.3 BFTS also arrived at the same time, but started training at the Spartan School of Aeronautics in Tulsa until the new school in Miami, Oklahoma, could be built. No.5 BFTS moved to Clewiston, Florida, in October 1941, after the first two courses began training in Arcadia, Florida. No.6 BFTS in Ponca City, Oklahoma, experienced delays in finding a suitable location. Several sites were proposed and rejected. Course 1 at No.6 BFTS arrived in August 1941, the same time as the third course arrived at the first schools.[18]

Even though the various BFTS schools experienced similar growing pains, certain unique characteristics developed. Students in

California spent their weekends in Hollywood. Students in Arizona were advised to check the cockpits of the training aircraft for rattle-snakes before the first flight each morning. Students in Florida flew over citrus groves scented by orange blossoms, while the school taught survival techniques and developed a search and rescue service due to its proximity to the inhospitable Everglades.

In Dallas, ground school classes, held in the Dallas Aviation School facilities at Love Field, began on June 3, the day after the initial cadets arrived.[19] The two ground school classrooms were located in a wooden building with a corrugated metal roof and offered limited accommodations, poor ventilation, and few amenities. Furnishings consisted of little more than tables or chairs with a small writing surface (such as found in local public schools) and a blackboard.

Luckey's efforts with the Army Air Corps supply system paid off three days later when the army delivered seventeen PT-18 primary trainers to the school. Heavy rains, high winds, and low clouds delayed the start of flight training, originally scheduled to begin on Monday, June 9. As torrents of rain fell from leaden skies, local creeks and rivers rose, then overflowed their banks. The rains prompted the RAF officers to comment that an earlier assertion by Major Long that Texas had 364 days of flying weather per year, "erred on the side of optimism."[20]

The skies cleared on Wednesday, June 11, 1941, and the sun shown brightly in the blue sky as A Flight of Course 1 assembled on the flight line at Dallas Love Field to meet their instructors and the aircraft in which they would learn to fly. The course of fifty students had been divided into two sections, A Flight and B Flight. Each flight spent half of each day in ground school and the other half flying. While one flight flew in the morning, the other flight attended ground school. In the afternoon the schedule reversed. This practical and efficient system continued for the duration of the school.

To the cadets, many of whom had never been in an airplane, the PT-18 presented an imposing sight. Officially the Boeing PT-18

Kaydet, the trainer had been designed by Lloyd Stearman in the mid-1930s as the Model 75 and originally manufactured by the Stearman Aircraft Company before the company became a division of Boeing Aircraft. A large open cockpit, fabric-covered biplane, known forever as simply the Stearman, the PT-18 towered over nine feet to the top of the upper wing and mounted an uncowled Jacobs R-755 seven-cylinder air-cooled radial engine developing 225 horsepower. The Stearman cruised at 106 miles per hour, landing approaches were flown at a sedate 65 miles per hour, and the trainer landed at 52 miles per hour.[21]

Even though noted for its easy handling in the air and rugged construction, the Stearman could be difficult to land, especially in a stiff cross wind. The Stearman acquired the nickname "yellow peril" from the navy's all yellow paint scheme and the aircraft's tendency to ground loop if not properly handled on landing. A ground loop is a fast, rather violent, rotation in a small circle on the ground, or as pilots would say, "the tail tried to swap places with the nose."

When the school reached full capacity, fifty instructors comprised the flight training staff. Each instructor had four students. The instructors were divided into flights of six primary instructors. Each flight also had a dispatcher to schedule student flights, keep track of each student's flight hours, and insure proper aircraft utilization.

The flight instructors were mostly young men, many not much older than the British cadets. But the majority of the instructors had considerable flying experience; some had learned to fly as teenagers, others with the army, and many had earned a living as crop dusters or in other risky aerial pursuits. Most of the instructors were from the southern United States and spoke in a slow drawl almost unintelligible to the young British students. The cadets also spoke in a variety of regional British accents that further confused matters.

Besides the unfamiliar speech, terminology offered a further challenge with terms such as fuel or gasoline instead of petrol, landing gear instead of undercarriage, and landing patterns instead of circuits. The aircraft were even referred to as ships, which seemed strange indeed. One later story, which could have originated with any of the schools, has an instructor explaining a maneuver before a flight and concluding by telling the student, "then give her the gun" meaning to advance the throttle and apply full power, whereupon the student looked confused and then replied slowly, "Sir we're not allowed to have guns in England."[22] After the British students became acclimated to the new jargon, most of this American terminology had to be discarded when the students graduated and returned to Britain and operational flying with the RAF.

In the air these problems were compounded by the communication system of the Stearman, which consisted of a flexible rubber tube called a gosport. The gosport allowed only one-way communication (usually garbled) from the instructor in the front cockpit to the student in the rear cockpit. Even though instructors usually discussed the flight session before takeoff, once in the air the student had no means of replying or asking questions.[23] With the roar of the unmuffled engine, the noise of the slipstream around the open cockpit, the limitations of the gosport, and the use of unfamiliar terminology spoken in a strange drawl, it is amazing so many students actually learned to fly. The Stearman, despite its imposing appearance, proved to be an excellent trainer.

The instructors began the familiarization phase of flight training with a walk around the aircraft pointing out the various aspects of the Stearman, including the engine, metal ground adjustable propeller, fuel tank (located in the center section of the top wing), oil reservoir, control surfaces, landing gear, streamlined wires which interconnected between the top and bottom wings, and instrumentation. After this introduction, each student would be responsible for performing an inspection of the aircraft before each flight.

After the walk around and introduction, the first student from each section climbed into the rear cockpit, a cavernous hole in the large round fuselage with a metal bucket seat and wide restraining belt. The seat had no cushion; each student sat on his own low-slung parachute. An instrument panel in front of the student contained only basic instruments: an airspeed indicator, altimeter, turn and bank indicator, oil pressure and oil temperature gauges, magnetic compass, tachometer, and a magneto switch. Two widely spaced rudder pedals were mounted on the floor below the instrument panel. Steel cables led from the rudder pedals to the rudder on the tail of the aircraft. The throttle and fuel mixture control were mounted on the left side of the cockpit. A wooden control stick jutted up from the floor between the student's legs. Steel cables running through various pulleys and fairleads led from the stick to the ailerons on the trailing edge of the lower wings and the elevators on the rear of the horizontal stabilizers at the tail of the aircraft.

From the cockpit, the arrangement of control cables and the Stearman's structure of welded steel tubing, painted liberally with green zinc chromate primer, were clearly visible. Oddly enough, considering the round shape of the fuselage, the welded steel tubing formed a square truss. Highly varnished wood stringers and formers attached to the steel tubing gave the Stearman's fuselage its round shape. Grade A cotton fabric, coated with multiple layers of nitrate dope to tauten and provide strength to the cotton, formed the exterior skin of the Stearman. The final coats of dope contained pigment that gave color to the aircraft's exterior.

The Stearman had no electrical system and relied on an inertia starter to start the engine. After both the instructor and the student climbed into the aircraft, a ground crewman mounted a step on the left side of the fuselage just behind the engine, inserted a metal crank into a receptacle connected to a heavy internal flywheel, and began to turn. The heavy flywheel spun faster and faster until the crewman removed the crank and pulled a T-shaped handle, which engaged the spinning flywheel with the engine's crankshaft. The flywheel imparted sufficient inertia to turn the engine over several times. Two independent magnetos fired two spark plugs in each cylinder, which started the engine.

Air-cooled radial engines (as opposed to in-line liquid cooled engines) were built with greater clearances between internal parts to allow for heat expansion, which also allowed a small amount of oil to drain past the lower cylinder rings after the engine had been shut down. When the engine started, this residue of oil quickly burned, producing an initial cloud of blue-grey smoke, which blew back and dissolved into the slipstream of the spinning propeller.

In 1941 the RAF system of pilot training consisted of two stages: elementary and advanced. The United States Army and Navy used a three-tiered system of pilot training in which students progressed from primary, to basic, and then advanced. In the army and navy systems, each stage of flight training utilized a different aircraft, each more sophisticated than the earlier trainer. Due to a shortage of advanced trainers, early courses in Terrell combined both the RAF and the United States systems. While following the RAF flight training syllabus, the Terrell program used three different levels (primary, basic, and advanced) and three different trainers as in the United States system.[24]

The RAF considered 150 hours—70 hours of elementary and 80 hours of advanced—to be the minimum flight time required to train a new pilot.[25] RAF officials anticipated that the efficiency of the BFTS All Through Training Scheme, which combined all phases of pilot training at one location (as opposed to the other training schemes in which students moved to a new base after completing each level of training), would allow students to achieve approximately 180 hours of flight time during the twenty weeks of training. In addition, the RAF planners anticipated the extra flight time could be achieved in the basic and advanced stages.

The student's first flight involved a kaleidoscope of emotions, sights, and sounds, beginning with the roar of the engine advanced to full power. After an incredibly short takeoff run the Stearman did not seem so much to fly, as the ground appeared to fall away from the aircraft as objects below grew smaller and smaller. As the Stearman climbed away from the airfield and the city of Dallas, the wings framed an ever expanding horizon of blue sky and white puffy clouds above a land interlaced with farm fields, forests, meandering creeks, and neatly laid out towns, all connected by a latticework of roads and country lanes. After a short while, the wings tilted, or rather the horizon seemed to slant, as the Stearman banked for the first time. These sights and sounds were forever indelibly imprinted into the student's mind, even more so than he realized at the time.

Early flights introduced the student to the fundamentals of flying and prepared him for solo. The student progressed from straight and level flight, to basic maneuvers such as shallow turns, climbs, descents, and stalls. Repetitious takeoffs and landings were practiced, and finally spins were introduced before the student's first solo. A spin is a prolonged stall in which the aircraft rotates rapidly around its center of gravity, with the nose well below the horizon, while it descends. Due to the disorienting nature of a spin and a propensity for the rotation to increase if not checked, spins were begun at a high enough altitude to insure recovery by 3,000 feet above the ground.

The first milestone in the evolution from student to fully rated pilot came with the student's first solo. Due to the heavy traffic around Love Field, training flights were conducted from a grass auxiliary field located three miles north of Love Field. The student's first solo occurred from the auxiliary field and usually consisted of two circuits around the pattern with two takeoffs and two landings. Students in Course 1 averaged just over twelve hours of flight time before their first solo.[26]

By the end of the first week in July, five cadets of Course 1 had been eliminated or washed out; three students were washed out before solo and two students just after solo. A basic lack of flying aptitude resulted in the majority of failures during primary training. Most of the civilian instructors in the BFTS schools worked to develop a bond with students and tried to insure the success of each student. This attitude contrasted sharply with the harsh discipline and hazing employed in the Arnold Scheme and to a lesser extent in the Towers Scheme, which was not only unfamiliar, but offensive to the British students.[27] In some cases cadets who washed out of Arnold Scheme schools were allowed to join a BFTS. In January 1942 three ex-Arnold Scheme students joined Course 7 in Terrell.[28]

After solo, students alternated between dual flights with the instructor and solo flights to practice airmanship. Of the minimum seventy hours in primary, the RAF flight syllabus anticipated that half of the time would be solo and half dual instruction. The dual instruction also included eight hours of instrument instruction.

Following solo, instructors introduced students to additional maneuvers including sideslips, a maneuver in which the ailerons and rudder are crossed (i.e., ailerons to turn the aircraft in one direction, countered by rudder in the opposite direction). This allows an aircraft on a landing approach to a short field to lose altitude rapidly without gaining airspeed. Sideslips are particularly valuable in aircraft such as the Stearman that do not have flaps. Students also practiced steep turns, chandelles, precautionary landings, low flying (always with an instructor, according to the regulations), and basic aerobatics such as loops, slow rolls, and Immelmanns.[29]

Even though the school syllabus followed the standard RAF flight syllabus, the instructors invariably added maneuvers from their civilian experience. These maneuvers usually involved some form of pylon 8 or S turns across a road. In a pylon 8 the aircraft traces a figure 8 at low altitude around two fixed objects on the ground such as trees or grain silos. With the wind at right angles to the figure 8 the purpose of the maneuver is to maintain a fixed distance from the objects on the ground while constantly turning the aircraft. In order to maintain the prescribed distance from the objects on the ground the student must always vary the angle of bank to compensate for the wind. Turns that transcribed a figure S across a road with the wind again at right angles to the road accomplished the same purpose.[30] The RAF saw little need for pylon 8s and S turns across a road, but these maneuvers taught students the value of proper coordination between the aircraft's rudder and ailerons.

After the principles of basic airmanship had become familiar, students embarked on cross-country flights. The first cross-country flight consisted of a flight and landing at another airport only thirty-five to forty miles away. The next cross-country flight involved a flight to an airport seventy-five to eighty miles away, a landing, and return. The third cross-country flight usually involved a triangular course, to test the student's ability to recognize and compensate for the effects of winds aloft on each leg of the flight and to avoid flying over the same leg.[31]

As flying progressed, ground school classes covered subjects such as armament, airframes, engines, law and discipline, aircraft maintenance, and airmanship lectures. A major portion of ground school involved classes in navigation and meteorology. Air navigation included the use of aerial charts, plotting wind triangles to determine course correction for the effects of winds aloft, and the use of the Dalton computer. A portable circular slide rule for determining course corrections for various winds aloft, the Dalton also provided ground speed over a course, true airspeed, fuel consumption, and solved time and distance problems.[32]

Meteorology delved into the mysterious world of air masses and frontal systems. Students also had to be proficient in signals, including the use of the aircraft radio (installed only in the basic and advanced trainers), and sending Morse code with both keys and signal lamps, known as Aldis lamps. Tests were scheduled throughout the course, and at the end of ground school students took a comprehensive written test called the Wings Examination.

The RAF recognized the importance of training in Link trainers, a forerunner of the modern flight simulator, and planned the Terrell school to include facilities for several Link trainers. The Link trainer consisted of a small plywood enclosure mounted on a short pedestal. The Link, which sported small mock wings, tail surfaces, and army dark blue paint, strongly resembled a penny arcade ride.[33] Designed for instrument training, the Link had no outside visual references, but did have full 360-degree turning movement and partial pitching movement. The cramped, dimly lit interior of the Link replicated a fully functioning aircraft instrument panel, control stick, and rudder pedals. An operator at a nearby panel controlled electrical inputs to the trainer. But the Link was not a toy, and an operator's fiendish manipulation of cross-winds and headings could leave the student, wrestling with con-trols in the darkened enclosure, shaken and sweating. A graph recorded the results of the Link session for later study.[34]

The sole Link trainer at the Dallas Aviation School had limited instrumentation compared to later models. Braniff Airways at Love Field had one of the latest model Link trainers and Luckey arranged for its use by the school. Students soon began training on both Link trainers. The contract between the school and the RAF speci-fied a fixed charge of $5.00 per hour for time in the Link trainer. Beveridge recommended that the hourly rate paid by the British for the Dallas Aviation School Link trainer should be less than that paid for the Braniff Link trainer due to the Dallas Aviation Link's reduced capabilities.[35]

During June and July, the school continued to be plagued by bad weather and equipment shortages.[36] Most of the items were relatively minor, but their absence resulted in delays and frustra-tion. A lack of tachometers grounded several of the Stearmans. Luckey had been able to procure lightweight cotton flight suits, but the woolen underwear and socks issued to the first cadets in Canada resulted in heat rashes. Goggles supplied to the cadets had clear lenses and resulted in headaches from the intense glare of the Texas sun. The RAF staff recommended tinted goggles, but the RAF Delegation in Washington replied, "It has generally been agreed that tinted glasses, though desirable, are not essential and therefore at present no Government issue will be made."[37] Because of the great distance from normal RAF base facilities, ordinary items such as clothing and shoe repairs were unavailable. The RAF staff requested, and received, an allowance to provide for these expenses.

Routine medical facilities, normally found on RAF bases, were also not available in Dallas and the RAF Delegation in Washington requested a local doctor to be on call. The RAF officers in Dallas retained a Dr. Williams for $450 per month to provide a qualified doctor for the school. Dr. Williams contracted with Dr. Oliver A.

Fulcher, a newly licensed physician, whom he paid $300 per month. Dr. Fulcher proved to be not only competent, but also popular with the cadets. Since he had no established practice, Dr. Fulcher agreed to move with the school to Terrell. Not only would the RAF retain the services of an excellent and popular doctor, but the move would also save the RAF Dr. Williams' $150 per month override fee.[38]

Shortly after training commenced in Dallas, Wing Commander Hilton assumed additional duties with No.3 BFTS, temporarily located in Tulsa, Oklahoma, and later with No.6 BFTS in Ponca City, Oklahoma. This situation resulted in Hilton's absence from Dallas much of the time and Beveridge assumed nominal command of No.1 BFTS.[39] It also became clear that additional staff would be necessary and Beveridge requested an armament NCO and an administrative officer. The armament NCO would lecture and also act as the station disciplinary sergeant major. A civilian secretary for the school, although authorized, proved difficult to hire because the officers wanted someone willing to move from Dallas to Terrell when the school relocated rather than train a new person in a couple of months.

As the army had already discovered, primary flight training out of Love Field had decided disadvantages. In addition to the congested flight conditions, the Dallas Aviation School classrooms were limited, and the wooden barracks with corrugated metal roofs, divided into small rooms that housed four cadets each, suffered from poor ventilation.[40] Many of the British cadets had difficulty sleeping in the barracks during the hot Texas summer nights.

Sports and recreation facilities were also not available at Love Field. The RAF officers inquired into a group membership at the local YMCA, but distances to the facilities, the severe time constraints of the training schedule, and a lack of any school transportation rendered the proposal impractical.

The early problems with equipment shortages, lack of supplies, limited facilities, and the weather were either solved or endured. A totally unexpected aspect of life in Dallas, however, surfaced. From the arrival of the first cadets, the British flight training program became the subject of intense local interest and press coverage. Hilton and Beveridge were besieged with requests for interviews, cadets posed for numerous photographs, and invitations poured into the school for cadets to visit local homes. The British officers reported, "Tremendous interest has been shown in us, and we have been overwhelmed with hospitality and offers of hospitality for ourselves and the pupils."[41]

Ever sensitive to local opinion, Hilton and Beveridge tried to accommodate the avalanche of requests on some sort of reasonable basis. Cadets were free to leave the school (known as open post) and go into town one weekday evening (usually Wednesday from 6:00 to 10:00 P.M.) and on weekends after noon on Saturday, subject to the flying schedule. Besides the press and individuals, local organizations also took an interest in the British cadets.

Even before the announcement of RAF training in the United States, several North Texas cities, including Dallas and Terrell, established War Relief Societies. These societies, made up of local women, raised money to aid civilians in Britain left homeless by bombings, gathered clothing and other donated articles, and knitted items such as sweaters and socks for British servicemen. Both the Dallas and Terrell War Relief Societies would be strong supporters of the British cadets throughout the duration of the school.

On June 16 the Dallas chapter of the British War Relief Society hosted the British cadets to a tour of their facilities at 1403 Elm Street in Dallas and provided a luncheon afterwards.[42] This occasion, as well as similar promotional events, generated considerable press attention.

The RAF officers attempted to handle unusual requests from the public with tact and diplomacy, but were often unsuccessful. When one couple from the affluent north Dallas suburb of Highland Park asked if the entire student class could attend a cook-out and swim party at their home, the officers replied that, unfortunately, the school had no transportation facilities and thought that ended the matter. The following Saturday morning fifteen Dallas taxicabs, hired by the couple, arrived at Love Field and transported the entire class to Highland Park.[43]

The interest shown in the British cadets extended beyond the local area. One weekend, the citizens of Henderson in Rusk County, 120 miles southeast of Dallas, gave the cadets a tour of an East Texas oil field, followed by a cook-out and dance. The city even sent a bus to Dallas to pick up the cadets. The public attention became so intense that Hilton and Beveridge began to wonder if what they termed, "This silly hero worship they had received at the hands of well-meaning Americans," might be detrimental to discipline and the good of the service.[44]

On July 19, 1941, Course 2, consisting of 49 cadets, arrived in Dallas. Three cadets from Course 1 were held back and joined Course 2. Cadets were held back for various reasons, the most common being illness that interrupted training. In the early courses slow students were sometimes held back. These cadets had not progressed at the same rate as the other students, but still exhibited sufficient promise to continue training. The day before Course 2 arrived, the army delivered eight more PT-18s to Love Field from Randolph Field in San Antonio.[45]

On the first day of flight training for Course 2, the RAF officers, who by this time must have felt they had encountered every conceivable problem, faced something entirely new. After the first flight, two cadets, who had never been in an airplane before, announced they did not like flying! This pronouncement came after the cadets had been recruited in England, transported across the North Atlantic, issued U.S. visas in Canada, and traveled across the United States to Dallas. Nothing could be done except ship the two cadets back to Canada for reassignment.

The Dallas RAF staff very sensibly recommended to the RAF Delegation in Washington that in the future, potential cadets in England should at least be given a ride in an airplane before undertaking the 5,000-mile journey to Texas. Group Captain Carnegie replied, "It is not practical to give a short flight in England to students, even those who have never been in an airplane."[46] Carnegie also stated that this situation had never occurred before and obviously considered the matter unique. Unique or not, this subject would come up again.

On July 25, the new administrative officer, Flt. Lt. M. W. Palmer, arrived in Dallas.[47] Familiar with RAF training commands, Palmer had been an instructor at an ITW unit. Palmer, a talented musician, composer, and singer, also had an engaging personality, which proved popular with the young cadets. Beveridge, although an intelligent and efficient officer, was a dour, somewhat straitlaced Scotsman and a non-flyer. He had never been particularly popular with the cadets.[48] Three weeks later on August 13, Sgt. C. E. Moffat, the new armament NCO, arrived in Dallas. The three officers—Hilton, the combat veteran, the efficient Beveridge, and the popular and outgoing Palmer—along with the newly arrived Moffat, formed an excellent team.

By the first week in August, the RAF staff reported, somewhat optimistically, that in spite of poor weather and equipment shortages, the students of Course 1 had completed three solo cross-country flights, eight hours of instrument flying, some formation flying, and rated the general ability of the class as high.[49] Unfortunately no night flying had been accomplished due to a lack of suitably equipped aircraft. Time in the Link trainer had been limited to about two hours per student. Nine students had been eliminated, but the remaining cadets would complete the seventy hours required in primary training by the end of the first week in August, which would be ahead of schedule. The RAF staff recommended that the cadets of Course 1 receive a week's leave following the completion of primary training in order "to maintain morale and enthusiasm."[50] The RAF Delegation in Washington approved this sensible recommendation and leave after primary remained in effect for the duration of the school, although the length of the leave varied slightly.

After Course 2 arrived, the Dallas Aviation School facility at Love Field reached full capacity. During the summer of 1941, Luckey divided his time between the operation of the Dallas school and supervising construction of the new Terrell facility. Beveridge frequently inspected the construction work, occasionally accompanied by Hilton. Course 3, scheduled to arrive in Texas sometime after the middle of August, had already been routed directly to Terrell and the school staff and RAF officers looked forward to moving into their permanent home.

---

1. There is a contradiction here since the British generally considered American flight training to be inferior. Air Commodore Pirie summed up this attitude in a letter dated 7 April 1941 to the Air Ministry, "the standard of training in this country (USA) is not as good as ours by a long way. . . . the American thinks that everything in America is superior to everything in any other country and one has to play up to this vanity—or is it inferiority complex?" AIR 20/1388.

2. "Permanent Historical Record, Royal Air Force Operations Record Book, Form 540, Headquarters Air Historical Branch, Air Ministry, London, No.1 British Flying Training School, Texas, USA." May 31, 1941. Located in the Public Record Office, London. Hereafter referred to as ORB.

3. ORB, June 2, 1941.

4. Ibid.

5. Ibid.

6. *Terrell Daily Tribune*, April 18, 1941.

7. ORB, June 2, 1941.

8. War Department, Air Corps Materiel Division, Memorandum 24-41A, dated June 6, 1941. Copy located in ORB, June 1941.

9. "A System of Elementary Flying Training," Air Ministry, London, publication, April 1941, contained in ORB.

10. The *Pasteur* lasted for over forty years in various roles and under various ownerships until it sank in the Indian Ocean in 1980 while being towed to Taiwan to be scrapped.

11. Jim Forteith, letter to the author, January 20, 2000.

12. Ibid. Jim Forteith altered his birth certificate in order to join the RAF at seventeen. He was one of the youngest, if not the youngest student to train in Terrell. Course 9 also contained Ray England, who at twenty-seven was one of the oldest students to train in Terrell.

13. A *New York Times* article on May 20, 1941, reported that British civilians soon to arrive in the United States to learn to fly were later destined for the RAF.

14. "Notes for the Guidance of Airmen Trainees Selected for Pilot and Observer Training at Certain Training Centers Overseas." Located in ORB.

15. ORB, June 2, 1941.

16. For an interesting look at a group of British cadets traveling to join an Arnold Scheme school see, Mark Murphy, "Journey from Moncton," *New Yorker* (October 30, 1943), 46-54.

17. ORB, June 2, 1941, also *Dallas Morning News,* June 3, 1941.

18. Dr. Gilbert S. Guinn, letter to the author, November 3, 2002.

19. ORB, June 7, 1941.

20. Ibid., June 14, 1941.

21. The army accepted the same aircraft with different engines under different designations. The PT-13 mounted a Lycoming R-680 radial engine of 220 horsepower and the PT-17 mounted a Continental R-670 radial engine of 220 horsepower. The navy also used the Stearman with slight modifications as the N2S. *Jane's Fighting Aircraft of WW II* (London: Jane's Publishing Company, 1946; reprint, Singapore: Random House, 1994), 211-12.

22. Davenport Steward, "As the English See Us: John Bull Explains the American Way to the RAF Abroad," *Saturday Evening Post* (October 11, 1941): 24.

23. Joe James, *Teacher Wore a Parachute* (New York: A.S. Barnes and Company, 1966), 16-18. The RAF found the gosport's one-way communication unacceptable. The army did not share the RAF's concern and the civilian schools were reluctant to make modifications to the systems without army approval. Finally the RAF procured British systems from supply centers in Canada. These modifications were not completed until early 1943. The complete correspondence relating to this matter is found in the Public Record Office (London) file 70837 Reference 45/15.

24. Guinn, "British Aircrew Training," 12.

25. Ibid., 10. Also ORB, Attachment dated December 27, 1941, 181.

26. ORB, 142. This is the final class report. An earlier report dated June 30, 1941, lists the average time to solo as 13 hours and 25 minutes and another report dated July 18, 1941, lists the average time to solo as 12 hours and 52 minutes. These discrepancies probably arise from the exclusion of those cadets who were later eliminated.

27. For a good example of the British attitude toward flight instruction see the story of one of England's greatest World War II fighter pilots, Robert Stanford Tuck, learning to fly in: Larry Forrester, *Fly For Your Life* (New York: Bantam Books, 1978), 31-36.

28. At one time the wash-out rate at Arnold scheme schools was reported to be twice that of the BFTS schools. Will Largent, *RAF Wings Over Florida: Memories of World War II British Cadets* (West Lafayette, Indiana: Purdue University Press, 2000), 17. Guinn, "British Aircrew Training," 12.

29. An Immelmann is a half loop with a half roll at the top popularized by World War I German ace Max Immelmann.

30. Bill Brookover, interview by the author, Granbury, Texas, January 9, 2000.

31. Fortnightly report from Beveridge to the RAF Delegation in Washington, D.C., dated August 1, 1941. Located as an attachment to ORB.

32. Phillip Dalton created his "Dalton Dead Reckoning Computer" around 1932. Later versions known as the E6-B were still in production and widespread use at the beginning of the twenty-first century.

33. In the early 1930s, Edwin Link, unable to interest the military, sold his first machines to amusement parks.

34. A November 16, 1941, *Terrell Daily Tribune* article has a good description of the operation of the Link Trainer.

35. ORB, July 18, 1941.

36. During the first year of the school's operation, East Texas experienced more than 50 inches of rainfall, as opposed to the normal annual average of approximately 39 inches. The *Texas Almanac, 2000-2001*, lists 1941 as officially the wettest year in Texas history.

37. ORB, July 13, 1941.

38. Ibid., June 9, 1941.

39. This situation has led to some confusion and several later sources refer to Beveridge as the first commanding officer.

40. These rooms were originally designed to house three army cadets each.

41. Dr. Gilbert S. Guinn, unpublished manuscript titled, "BFTS No.1 The Influence of Events" in the possession of the author.

42. *Dallas Morning News*, June 17, 1941.

43. ORB, June 9, 1941.

44. Ibid., Course 1 final report November 2, 1941.

45. Ibid., July 18, 1941.

46. Letter dated August 5, 1941, from Carnegie to Beveridge, located in ORB, August 1941.

47. ORB, July 25, 1941.

48. Bert Allam, letter to the author, November 30, 1999.

49. Fortnightly report dated August 1, 1941, from Beveridge to the RAF Delegation in Washington, D.C. Located as an attachment to ORB.

50. ORB, August 1, 1941.

As soon as Major Long and Terrell city officials signed the agreement on June 14, 1941, construction of the airport got underway. At the same time, Terrell citizens launched a vigorous campaign to ensure passage of the countywide bond election to be held on June 28. More than one hundred Terrell volunteers canvassed the county speaking to various groups.

Airport supporters presented a two-pronged message: support of the airport would be good economically and would also be patriotic. The headline of one full-page newspaper advertisement asked, "Is Your Son's Life Worth 16 Cents a Year?" The ad went on, "Can you deny the vital importance of training British RAF flyers on U.S. soil in Kaufman County as a step toward keeping your own son far from war-torn bomb-shattered lands?" and "Can any red-blooded citizen of Kaufman County afford to ignore even the smallest opportunity to insure our American way of life?"[1] At a mass meeting, Kaufman mayor Emmett Day commented, "In times like these we must forget petty differences and unite in this nation-wide, democracy-wide undertaking."[2]

Despite the campaign, considerable opposition to the airport surfaced. Editor Mike Boggess of the *Kemp News* wrote, "Terrell will be the town that reaps the benefits and it seems from this distance that Terrell should foot the bill."[3] Irate Terrell civic leaders angrily denounced the opposition as, "subversive elements, who would defeat the issue in the interest of Nazi Germany," and "enemies of democracy."[4] Emotions ran so high that in several instances Terrell residents who called on stores and businesses in south Kaufman County to discuss the bond issue were asked to leave.

The county bond issue passed by a slim margin of 214 votes, with 1,675 votes cast in favor of the bonds and 1,461 votes against. Terrell voters approved the bonds by an overwhelming ninety-five percent margin. Kaufman voters were split with a slight majority voting against the bonds. Other Kaufman County precincts voted heavily against the bond issue. In Mabank, at the opposite end of Kaufman County, eighty-three percent voted against the bonds. In Kemp, twenty-five miles southeast of Terrell, and Crandall, fifteen miles southwest, eighty percent voted against the bonds. In the small community of Whitehall, in far southeast Kaufman County, all sixteen registered voters voted against the bonds.

Commenting on the election results, editor Boggess of the *Kemp News* sourly predicted, "When it is over we will have 526 acres of land owned by the county that will be something for Kaufman County politicians to wrangle over." The editor of the *Mabank Banner* stated emphatically, "The bond issue was not a question of national defense."[5] Following the election, emotions remained high and no representative of any Kaufman County town, except Terrell and Kaufman, attended the official airport groundbreaking ceremony on June 30, 1941. At the ceremony, held under a hot, clear blue summer sky, T. Killian McElroy, chairman of the Terrell city commission, presided, Major Long and County Judge Ashworth turned the first spades of dirt, county commissioners were introduced, others including bank president W. P. Allen said a few words, the Terrell municipal band played patriotic tunes, and Beveridge thanked the enthusiastic crowd, "On behalf of myself, my service, and my country."[6]

By the middle of July, work was well underway on the first six buildings for the new school, which included the main administration building, mess hall and canteen, two barracks, and two ground school buildings with classrooms. Trucks, as well as mule-drawn wagons, delivered materials to the construction site. From the administration building, located just inside the entrance to the airfield, a single wide sidewalk led to the southeast with the mess hall on one side of the sidewalk, followed by the two ground school buildings, one on either side of the sidewalk, and then the two barracks, again with one on either side of the sidewalk. The barracks were 120 feet long by 30 feet wide and, influenced by the Love Field experience, were open on the inside with numerous exterior windows for ventilation.[7] Two-tiered bunks were arranged along each wall and small lockers provided space for personal items. The center section of each barracks contained shower and toilet facilities. Each of the barracks housed two courses, with each course of fifty cadets occupying one end of the barracks.

Even though the British students found the school facilities neat, well arranged, and generally above average by the military standards of the day, the open lavatories offered a surprise. Sinks and toilets were arranged in long lines with no partitions of any kind. Showers were taken in a large open area with shower heads spaced along the wall, again with no partitions. Almost all British students later remarked that inhibitions quickly became a thing of the past at Terrell and echoed the sentiments of Brian Latham of Course 19, "It (the barracks) really was very comfortable, but there was absolutely no privacy. Even the lavatories were in a row and you were shoulder to shoulder, chatting and straining amiably! It was no use being bashful."[8]

With the exception of two large steel frame hangars, all of the school buildings were of single-story wood construction built on concrete slab foundations. The buildings were located at the northwest corner of the airfield, near the dirt road leading into town. The remainder of the airport land angled to the southeast for approximately 1⅓ miles. The wide grass-covered area allowed takeoffs and landings in any direction from north-south to northwest-southeast (these directions conformed to the prevailing winds).

The school facilities, although neat and well arranged, reflected the austerity of Long's early flying experiences and the lasting impression of the Great Depression. Long had survived financial difficulties to become not only a respected flying school operator, but a tightfisted businessman. There were no hard surface runways or luxury items such as a swimming pool or prepared recreation facilities, other than a cleared area for calisthenics or group athletics such as football (soccer to Americans).[9] Based on surviving records, the RAF officers found the facilities entirely satisfactory, the food nutritious and plentiful, and the school staff competent and enthusiastic, which more than satisfied the urgent need to train pilots.

The only minor disagreement concerned the recreation hall, which had been included in the original plans. School officials decided not to build this building since they felt the students could use the barracks or canteen for any after hours activities such as studying and letter writing.[10] The RAF staff, however, felt that a recreation hall offered positive benefits, and Long had originally agreed to build the school in accordance with RAF preferences. The recreation hall was put back into the construction schedule, but the design now included a dispensary at one end. The dispensary had a waiting room for daily sick call and six beds. Due to the delay, the recreation hall would not be completed with the initial school buildings.

When completed, both the recreation hall and the canteen included wide screened-in verandas that allowed the passage of cooling summer breezes and the nocturnal noises of rural East Texas, which became so familiar to the British cadets. The still country nights carried sounds such as the far off barking of a dog, the occasional low rumble of a car passing in the distance, and the forlorn lament of a retreating train whistle, all mingled with the nearer sounds of night birds, the constant chirping of crickets, and the steady drone of insects. These sounds, blended with the fragrance of jasmine, honeysuckle, roses, and other growing things, would in the months and years to come leave an indelible impression on the young British students destined to train in Terrell.

The school also complied with the RAF staff's request for six ground school classrooms (considered excessive by army standards).[11] In addition, the RAF staff voiced concerns over the removal of grass and ground cover on the airfield by the grading and leveling process. Luckey agreed to sod these bare areas, but the RAF concerns later proved to be well-founded.

In addition to the work on buildings and site grading, Texas Power and Light Company started relocating the power line, which ran across the northwest corner of the field. The city also let contracts to extend water, sewer, and electrical lines to the airport.

Terrell officials requested federal aid from the Federal Works Agency in Fort Worth for extending the utility lines to the airport as a national defense measure under the Community Facility Act. The agency denied the request since the improvements were for training British pilots. Terrell municipal leaders promptly contacted Sam Rayburn, Speaker of the House of Representatives (not for the first time), and shortly afterward received assurances that the extension of utility lines to the airport did indeed fall under the provisions of the act. Rayburn concluded his letter to the chairman of the Terrell city commission, "If you have any further difficulty, please let me know, and I will do what I can."[12]

As the first six buildings neared completion, structural steel for the first of two large (204 feet long by 106 feet wide) hangars arrived on August 11 from Tulsa, Oklahoma. Heavy trucks moved the steel beams and roof trusses from the rail station in town to the airfield. At the airfield, special trucks fitted with hoisting devices lifted the steel beams and trusses into place.[13]

Crews also excavated for four 8,000-gallon underground fuel storage tanks located just east of the hangars. The primary trainers operated on 73-octane aviation fuel, while the basic and advanced trainers required 91-octane fuel.

Since the city had not received a bid for excavation from any contractor with power equipment, laborers dug the six to eight-foot deep trench to the airport for the water and sewer lines by hand. Falling behind on the excavation, the city authorized work to proceed seven days a week, and work schedules increased from eight hours to ten hours a day, but on regular pay without overtime.[14]

Major Long hired Wattie Sheppard, formerly in charge of the officers dining hall at Camp Bowie, located just outside Brownwood,

Texas, to supervise the mess hall. Meals would be served cafeteria style from a long serving line. Years later former British students would comment on the quantity and quality of the food served in the mess hall. Foods such as eggs, marmalade, sugar, fresh fruit, vegetables, juices, milk, including chocolate milk, and ice cream were especially welcome after the austerity and food rationing of wartime Britain. One end of the mess hall contained the canteen, which offered small items such as candy, chewing gum, and soft drinks from a soda fountain.

Equipment for the mess hall, including dishwashers, steam tables, ranges, and stainless steel tables, arrived on August 12. H. V. DesRochers, Long's purchasing agent, commented to a Terrell Rotary Club luncheon that army students at the Hicks Field location drank 2,200 half pints of milk each day.[15]

As construction on the new base progressed, Luckey and Dr. Fulcher inspected several clinics in Terrell. They decided that the Holton-Johnson clinic offered the most complete facilities, including a well-equipped surgery, conveniently located on the first floor.[16] Dr. L. W. Johnson, owner of the clinic, hired Dr. Fulcher. Either Dr. Johnson or Dr. Fulcher attended morning sick call at the school and then worked at the clinic afterwards. The RAF staff considered Dr. Johnson to be the senior medical officer for the school. Minor procedures for the British cadets were handled at the base dispensary; emergencies and more serious cases were taken to the clinic in town.

On the afternoon of August 13, 1941, as the school facilities neared completion, Terrell residents heard the sound of approaching aircraft. The sound grew louder and louder until a formation of twenty-three Vultee BT-13 trainers appeared in the blue summer sky and flew low over the town. The first contingent of basic trainers for the school had arrived from Goodfellow Army Airfield in San Angelo, Texas. Eleven of the planes were destined for Terrell; the other aircraft came to take the pilots back.[17]

On streets across the town, cars and trucks stopped or pulled over to the side of the road, merchants left shops and stores, and women abandoned household chores, picked up babies and went outside. Nearly everyone in town gazed upward into the clear sky. Each Vultee trainer sported the standard army dark blue fuselage, bright yellow wings, and red and white stripes on the rudder. The entire town reverberated to the collective roar of twenty-three low-flying trainers, each mounting a powerful Pratt and Whitney 450-horsepower radial engine. Each engine produced a distinctive throaty roar from its short exhaust stacks. People instinctively headed for the airport as each aircraft turned and entered the standard army line astern descending circular landing pattern developed in World War I.

Vehicles and pedestrians choked the one-lane dirt road leading to the airport and created the worst traffic jam in Terrell's history. Arriving cars pulled off the road and parked in nearby fields. Since the airport had no fence, the arriving citizens simply walked out onto the field as the aircraft landed. The still rough and uneven grass field had no defined runways or taxiways.

The Vultee BT-13 has a conventional landing gear consisting of two main wheels under the wings and a small tailwheel under the rear fuselage. On the ground, the aircraft sits with the nose in the air and the tail on the ground. This position and the round cowling enclosing the radial engine virtually eliminate the pilot's forward visibility while on the ground. In order to see ahead while taxiing, the pilot must constantly S-turn the aircraft.

As each plane landed, the pilots alternately craned their heads from side to side to see around the round noses, stabbed the rudder pedals and brakes to S-turn, while applying bursts of power to taxi over the uneven ground as local residents walked around to get a better look at the airplanes. Miraculously, the twenty-three trainers taxied into a rough line with a final burst of power, the engines were shut down, and the silver propellers slowly came to a stop without inflicting injury. The next day, Luckey diplomatically reminded Terrell residents to "Please be careful around the aircraft."[18] Two days later, four more BT-13s arrived.

Finishing touches to the initial buildings, including light fixtures, venetian blinds, ceiling fans, utensils and dishes for the mess hall, and the telephone system (phone number 960), were completed the next week, while work progressed on the hangars and utility lines to the airport. Several of the buildings featured interior walls paneled in natural knotty pine. Landscaping, including rosebushes along the new fence on both sides of the entrance gate, added the finishing touch to the uniform white buildings with green roofs. Cotton still grew next to several of the buildings, while both the United States and Royal Air Force flags flew from the flagpole in front of the administration building.

As the school buildings neared completion, county maintenance crews began work to widen the single-lane dirt road into town to a full thirty feet and then extend the road along the northern boundary of the airfield. This road carried all supplies for the school, including fuel from the Terrell train station to the airfield. City crews then added gravel to the city's portion of the widened road and county crews added gravel to the sections outside the city limits. Both government entities intended to add a coating of asphalt to the road at a later date.

Cadets from Course 1 returned from leave, and along with the cadets from Course 2, began moving on Saturday, August 23, from Dallas Love Field to the new Terrell facility. Instructors flew thirty Stearman PT-18 primary trainers and five BT-13 basic trainers from Dallas to Terrell over the weekend. Another Stearman flown by "Red" Vincell suffered an engine failure and made a forced landing without damage near Mesquite just east of Dallas.[19] Several instructors performed aerobatics before landing, which thrilled the throng of local citizens who had come to the airfield to watch the move. The canteen's soda fountain did a brisk business in the summer heat as the newly installed juke box played popular tunes.

Training began on Monday, August 25, although 4½ inches of rain that fell the previous day, postponed the start of flight operations. The new school buildings appeared to rise from a sea of mud. Cadets for Course 3 arrived in Terrell later in the week, after disappointed Terrell citizens met each arriving westbound train on Tuesday the previous week. The arrival schedule had been changed after publication in the local paper.[20]

During the move to Terrell, the school received four additional PT-18s, which completed the initial complement of thirty-five primary trainers (Stearmans) and twenty basic trainers (Vultee BT-13s).[21] The advanced trainers (twenty North American AT-6s) were not due to be delivered for another month, in time for Course 1 to begin advanced training. The daily availability of aircraft depended on serviceability and accidents. Aircraft that suffered minor damage were repaired locally by the school's civilian maintenance crews. Seriously damaged aircraft were disassembled and trucked to the Randolph Field repair facility in San Antonio. Aircraft destroyed in accidents were not always replaced immediately.

Soon after the move the cadets received open post and ventured into Terrell for the first time. They walked down streets, sometimes tying up traffic, and took in the small town sights and sounds. Cadets were amazed by the quantity and quality of products on store shelves, the numbers of large cars, and the town lights. Several places became well known to all those who trained in Terrell: a family owned flower shop and the two daughters, Virginia and Bertha Brewer, the Cris' cafe, the two cinemas, the Lyric and Iris, and the favorite meeting place, the Bass Drug store. The cadets had already been introduced in Dallas to the collective plural "y'all" used by Texans, but the open friendliness of Texans was still somewhat disconcerting to the reserved and shy young cadets. Townspeople greeted each other warmly, and even spoke to strangers on the street. Young girls in summer cotton dresses were seen and even said hello. The cadets quickly accepted this natural Texas hospitality.

In an effort to enhance school spirit, the RAF officers asked the cadets to submit suggestions for a school crest. Cadet Frank Miller, a former art student, created the design selected. The crest featured a shield divided into four equal parts. The four sections contained a British lion, an American eagle, two hands clasped in friendship, and a lone star, representing Texas. A belt, with the buckle and the words "1 BFTS" at the bottom, surrounded the shield. The belt contained the Latin inscription, *MARE NOS DIVIDIT. SED CAELA CONJUNGUNT* - *The Seas Divide and the Sky Unites.* A British royal crown topped the crest.

The RAF staff submitted the crest to the RAF Delegation in Washington for approval. Even though Group Captain Carnegie found that "The design and motto are considered to be most appropriate in every way," the school was not an established RAF unit. In addition, the approval of an official crest required payment of a registration fee, then considerable research by the RAF, and finally lengthy correspondence regarding details. Carnegie commented, "It would not surprise me if the war had terminated before the necessary formalities had eventually been completed," but then offered a practical suggestion. "My entirely private and unofficial advice is that you continue to use the crest until some objection is raised."[22] The staff adopted this sound advice.

The Terrell school used auxiliary fields to alleviate traffic congestion at the main airfield (the same system initially used at Love Field). Just after the middle of August, as the school buildings neared completion, Long entered into leases for two auxiliary fields. The first field contained 370 acres of the Gordon Tarver farm located fifteen miles southeast of the Terrell airfield. The second auxiliary field contained 250 acres of the E. N. Boykin farm, located five miles south of the airfield, midway between Terrell and Kaufman.[23]

Due to the different flight characteristics of the trainers such as landing speeds and pattern altitudes, each auxiliary field supported a specific type of training. Primary trainers used Boykin Field, while the basic and advanced trainers used Tarver Field. In addition to the leased auxiliary fields, the school frequently used the CAA field at Wills Point, located twenty miles east of Terrell.[24] This grass field northwest of Wills Point also had a rotating beacon for night flying.

Since the RAF staff officers were now fully involved in the operation of the school and not mere advisers, as the original concept had unwisely anticipated, the officers asked the RAF Delegation in

Washington for a copy of the contract with the civilian school operator.[25] This logical request would provide necessary guidelines for the working relationship between the civilian operators and the RAF staff. The Washington Delegation, however, did not feel it prudent to supply a copy of the contract, but realizing the practical benefits of the request, supplied a summary:

1. The operator's responsibility includes furnishing and maintaining equipment, auxiliary fields, supplies, and facilities required for training, except for airplanes, fuel, and oil, which would be supplied by the army under lend-lease guidelines.

2. The RAF has the authority to reject ground instructors.

3. The RAF has the authority to evaluate the flight proficiency of both students and instructors (this implies, but does not specifically grant, the authority to reject flight instructors).

4. The RAF is allowed to determine if aircraft are kept in a safe condition.

5. The RAF is allowed to make suggestions for improvement.

6. Parachutes must be repacked every sixty days.

7. Individual records of flight time will be kept by the school operator, but will be available for inspection and verification by the RAF staff.

8. The flight time charged by the school will be from the time the aircraft takes off until it returns to the flight line, less any time on the ground at other fields. Time will be kept to the nearest minute.

9. The cost of medical and dental care is a direct cost to the RAF. A request for these expenses to be included under lend-lease has not been resolved.

When No.1 BFTS opened in Terrell on August 25, 1941, the downtown Iris theater featured *Charley's Aunt* with Jack Benny. At the Lyric theater, *The Wagons Roll at Dawn* with Humphrey Bogart and Sylvia Sidney had just opened, admission ten cents. Martin Jarvis Garment offered men's tropical worsted suits with a choice of one or two pairs of pants for $22.50 and $25.00, the Robertson Grocery and Market sold bacon (wrapped) for twenty-five cents a pound, and the White Auto Store had Gillette tires, 6.00-16 size, for $9.45 each. The first bale of cotton for the season arrived in town and sold for seventeen cents a pound, a considerable improvement over the ten cents a pound paid the year before.

Even though many Terrell residents were hired to work at the school, other employees such as flight instructors, ground school instructors, and aircraft mechanics relocated to Terrell. The base housed only the RAF students; all others, including the RAF officers, lived in town. One estimate placed the number of new families at 150. With the influx of new workers at the school, Terrell experienced a housing shortage.

The editor of the *Terrell Daily Tribune* worried that some residents were taking advantage of the influx of new workers. In some cases, rent for houses which previously rented for thirty dollars per month had been raised to fifty dollars a month and some apartment rents had gone from twenty-five to forty dollars a month. Even though the editor admitted that these practices were confined to a small number, he reminded everyone that, "the automobile is here to stay" and if rents rose "beyond reason" people would simply commute from out of town.[26] Apparently these practices were not confined to landlords; Terrell barbers raised the price of a shave from twenty cents to twenty-five cents.

On August 26, 1941, the *Terrell Daily Tribune* published a special edition of the newspaper to commemorate the RAF presence. Virtually every business and organization in town took out advertisements. These ads all carried welcome messages, usually with patriotic themes. The city of Terrell's full-page ad featured a drawing of four diving Army Curtiss P-40 fighters and the huge headline "Welcome RAF." The American Bank ad proclaimed, "They're getting louder and louder—the throbbing, pulsing, beating roars of Democracy in the air. They speak louder than a dictator can shout, for they're the voice of free men." The Penny's department store ad slightly misquoted Winston Churchill's famous tribute to the RAF when it stated, "Never in the field of human conflict have so many owed so much to so few."[27] And a host of smaller ads such as: "RAF, We Welcome You" from the Terrell Laundry, "Welcome RAF" from the Bass Drug, and "We Welcome You RAF," from the Terrell Savings and Loan.[28]

Terrell residents immediately accepted the RAF cadets as their own. Invitations flooded into the school for cadets to join families for weekend meals and outings. Churches and other groups organized picnics. The American Legion hosted a dance; dances at the American Legion hut would become regular occurrences. The Terrell War Relief Society hosted a tea at Cris' Cafe. Cadets sat in a special reserved section of the grandstands for the local softball playoffs between Abner, Texas, and Elliot Lumber Company. The producers of a local play titled *Crazy House* encouraged local residents to take cadets to the performances as their guests.[29]

Although overwhelmed and gratified by the community enthusiasm, Beveridge tactfully reminded Terrell residents, "The cadets are here to work."[30]

1. *Terrell Daily Tribune,* June 26, 1941.

2. Ibid., June 11, 1941.

3. Ibid., July 5, 1941.

4. Ibid., June 27, 1941.

5. Ibid.

6. Ibid., July 1, 1941.

7. ORB, June 30, 1941.

8. Dr. Gilbert S. Guinn, compilation of student recollections.

9. A privately owned swimming pool and the Texas Military College, a private school in Terrell, offered the use of their facilities to the British cadets. The Works Progress Administration (WPA) also agreed to supply a part time physical training instructor. Records in ORB indicate this individual started on September 15, 1941, but it is not clear what became of this plan.

10. ORB, July 24, 1941.

11. Ibid., June 30, 1941.

12. *Terrell Daily Tribune,* August 7, 1941.

13. Ibid., August 15, 1941.

14. Ibid., August 16, 1941.

15. Ibid., August 14, 1941.

16. ORB, June 9, 1941.

17. *Terrell Daily Tribune*, August 15, 1941.

18. Ibid.

19. Severe vibration from a broken crankshaft threw the propeller and sheared all but one of the engine mounting bolts. A picture of school mechanics disassembling the Stearman with the engine hanging at a bizarre angle appeared in *Dallas Morning News* two days later. Vincell was killed after the war while crop dusting in Arkansas.

20. *Terrell Daily Tribune*, August 20, 1941.

21. ORB, August 23, 1941.

22. Letter dated September 30, 1941, from Carnegie to Beveridge located in ORB, September 1941.

23. This is the same land mentioned several times in earlier discussions with the Civil Aeronautics Authority as a possible county airport site.

24. ORB, September 25, 1941.

25. Fortnightly report from Hilton to Carnegie dated July 7, 1941, located in ORB. Carnegie's reply is dated July 13, 1941, and is located in the same file.

26. *Terrell Daily Tribune*, July 2, 1941.

27. After the Battle of Britain in the summer of 1940, Winston Churchill told the House of Commons, "Never in the field of human conflict was so much owed by so many to so few." Churchill, *Their Finest Hour*, 340.

28. *Terrell Daily Tribune*, August 26, 1941.

29. Ibid. August 25, 1941.

30. Ibid. August 23, 1941.

CHAPTER 4

By the end of the first week in September 1941, work on the first hangar had been completed. Both hangars had distinctive curved roofs with low shed-type structures along each side for maintenance shops, parts storage, and offices. Full-height sliding doors at each end of the hangars opened to allow unhindered access to the interior of the hangar. The control tower, a raised wood and glass enclosure constructed on metal legs and topped by a rotating beacon, stood at the southeast corner of the first hangar.[1]

Work progressed on the second hangar located to the east of the first hangar and the Link trainer building, located between the first hangar and the main school buildings. Due to the sensitive electronics, the Link trainer building was the only air-conditioned building on the base.[2] A fence encircled the airport complete with signs identifying the airport as government property. The county finished widening and graveling the road from town to the airport and along the northern boundary to the eastern edge of the field.

The cadets of Course 1 found the new basic trainer, the Vultee BT-13, to be very different from the Stearman.[3] Equipped with a more powerful 450-horsepower Pratt and Whitney R-985 nine-cylinder air-cooled radial engine, the BT-13, a low-wing monoplane, featured all metal construction (except for the control surfaces which were fabric-covered), a long sliding plexiglass canopy that enclosed the cockpit with its two tandem seats, a two-position adjustable propeller, manually operated wing flaps, and a fixed landing gear. The BT-13 had an electrical system that allowed amenities such as a starter for the engine, navigation and landing lights for

night flying, and a radio, including two-way communication between the student and the instructor. The Vultee cruised at 140
miles per hour and landed more than twenty miles per hour faster
than the Stearman.

Opinions regarding the Vultee trainer varied widely, and the BT-
13 never achieved the popularity of the Stearman.[4] Many instructors found the BT-13 to be underpowered; others questioned the
trainer's stall characteristics. The wildest rumors maintained that,
when stalled, the Vultee would always roll inverted. Actually, stalls
in the Vultee were normal when performed at altitude with the
wings level. When stalled out of a turn, however, the Vultee would
snap toward the high wing and the nose would pitch sharply down-
ward.[5] A stall in the Vultee at low altitude, such as on a landing
approach, especially out of an uncoordinated turn, could be deadly.
An experienced RAF pilot commented on the BT-13, "It has a tendency to snap roll on landing, which can be rather disconcerting.
Other than that it isn't very dangerous."[6]

Bert Allam of Course 4 noticed that his instructor flew the BT-13
straight and level and allowed Allam to solo the aircraft after only
a brief check out. Allam concluded the instructor actually feared
the Vultee. Allam, however, enjoyed flying the BT-13 and became
proficient in aerobatics, including spins, even though his instructor never demonstrated aerobatics in the BT-13.[7]

The five weeks of basic training involved transition to the more
sophisticated BT-13, but in other ways constituted a continuation of the airmanship skills learned in primary training. After
a thorough cockpit familiarization on the ground (not only valuable as a training tool, but cockpit drills on the ground did not
cost the RAF), the student usually flew with the instructor for
four or five hours and then soloed the BT-13. These flights involved familiar maneuvers in the new trainer such as climbs,
shallow and steep turns, stalls, basic aerobatics, and repetitive
takeoffs and landings. After solo, the student practiced maneuvers from the auxiliary field and set out on longer cross-country
flights.

During additional dual flights, students practiced flying in loose formations (usually three- or four-plane formations, since the RAF did not stress precision formation flying). With the full instrumentation of the basic trainer the student spent more time practicing instrument flying. Under the watchful eye of the instructor, the student flew solely by reference to the instruments while a canvas curtain covered the inside of the forward section of the canopy. The time spent flying from the main Terrell field to the auxiliary field or practice area provided an opportunity for flying on instruments or formation flying. Dual cross-country flights usually involved one leg on instruments. This combined navigation with climbs to cruising altitudes and maintaining various airspeeds and predetermined headings while on instruments.

Night flying began on September 11.[8] Several of the PT-18s had been modified for night flying by the addition of navigation and cockpit lights. The primary trainers were not equipped with landing lights or flares, usually considered necessary for night flying. Cadets received about two hours of dual instruction at night in the primary phase of training. At first, solo flights at night were not undertaken until basic training. Cadets in some later courses, however, did solo at night in the primary trainer. The field used smudge pots to mark takeoff and landing areas. Later courses had the benefit of a light bar installed in June 1942 at the end of the runway. A visible amber light indicated a high approach, a green light indicated a correct approach angle, and a red light indicated a low approach.

No amount of ground instruction could adequately prepare a low-time student for night flying. The first takeoff into a black sky was fraught with apprehension. During a night landing approach, descending into the darkness toward a dimly flickering row of smudge pots with the landscape and its associated obstacles and hazards shrouded in darkness, a student experienced a sense of foreboding that could quickly develop into fear if not controlled. Only the largest cities offered visual landmarks at night; smaller towns and villages usually extinguished their lights and disappeared into the darkness when the residents went to bed.

There were, however, moments of exquisite beauty when flying on a night cross-country under a clear sky illuminated by a full moon. These moments inspired quiet reflection and introspection. But these times were offset by the dread of flying into an unseen cloud front on a dark night when the student's first inclination of trouble came when the stars and the few lights on the ground disappeared. The worst fear concerned the possibility of an engine failure at night. Standard procedure in case of an engine failure at night was to bail out unless an airport was within gliding distance. One student successfully landed his aircraft after a night engine failure. Later the same student ran out of fuel at night and again attempted to land the aircraft. This time the student lost his life.

The RAF training syllabus emphasized the routine nature of night flying and instrument flying.[9] As late as the 1930s, military services in both the United States and England considered night flying and instrument flying to be specialized fields to be undertaken only by specially trained pilots in specially equipped aircraft.[10] At Terrell, night flights, instrument instruction, and time in the Link trainer were scheduled frequently for short intervals throughout flight training rather than all at once or in one or two long sessions.

The BFTS flight training program did not offer any training in multi-engine aircraft. To compensate for this limitation (which was obvious from the inception of the program), the RAF Delegation in Washington instructed the various schools to segregate basic and advanced students according to their likely future operational duties in the RAF. Students destined for multi-engine aircraft (bombers, transports, and coastal reconnaissance) were to receive more navigation and instrument instruction. Students destined for fighter command were to receive more training in aerobatics.[11] Determining a student's future operational status at this stage of training, especially with the available equipment, proved impossible. The RAF quickly discarded this plan in the BFTS program. The plan proved more successful at army schools in the Arnold Scheme where British students could be sent to either an army single engine or multi-engine base for advanced training.

On September 27, 1941, the school received five new AT-6 Harvard advanced trainers from the North American Aviation plant in Dallas.[12] Designed to approximate the characteristics of operational aircraft, the low-wing, all-metal (except for the control surfaces) AT-6 mounted a 550-horsepower Pratt and Whitney R-1340 nine-cylinder air-cooled radial engine (rated at 600-horsepower for takeoff), enclosed cockpit, full instrumentation, retractable landing gear, hydraulic wing flaps, landing lights, and a Hamilton Standard constant speed propeller. The AT-6 had a top speed of 210 miles per hour and cruised between 155 and 185 miles per hour, depending on the power settings.[13]

Chief advanced flight instructor E. Van Lloyd and several instructors designated to teach advanced flight in the AT-6 attended an instructor's course at Kelly Field in San Antonio. During the course, the army instructors made several negative comments concerning the North American trainer, especially regarding its spinning characteristics and its tendency to ground loop. These comments caused some misgivings among the instructors. Wing Commander Hilton allayed these fears by relating the favorable experiences of the British flight schools with the Harvard and even demonstrated various maneuvers in the aircraft (see Appendix B for a further review of this incident).

The concerns about the AT-6 expressed by the army instructors did have some basis in fact. Both the British and the Army Air Corps conducted extensive evaluations of the AT-6 and prohibited spins in the aircraft in late December 1941. The army and RAF lifted the spinning prohibition after North American strengthened the vertical stabilizer attachment fitting in the spring of 1942.[14] By July 1942, three of the AT-6s at Terrell had received the modification and were cleared for spins. On September 28, 1941, the remaining fifteen AT-6s of the initial complement of advanced trainers arrived in Terrell from Selma, Alabama.[15]

Although regarded as a forgiving and pleasant flying aircraft, and ultimately the favorite aircraft of almost every cadet, the AT-6 presented a formidable challenge to low-time students due to its higher operating speeds and more sophisticated systems. The landing approach in the Stearman had required not much more than retarding the throttle, setting up the appropriate glide speed, and aiming the aircraft at the runway. The AT-6, however, required lowering the landing gear, lowering the wing flaps, adjusting the trim, setting the propeller control, insuring the proper mixture and carburetor heat settings, and the selection of the reserve fuel tank (the AT-6 had two main fuel tanks and a reserve tank, each of which could be selected individually). In an era before printed check lists, students repeated the acronym TMPFF, which stood for trim, mixture, pitch, fuel, and flaps before each takeoff, and UMPFF, for undercarriage, mixture, pitch, fuel, and flaps, before each landing.

The advanced trainers flew the landing pattern at an altitude of 1,000 feet, as opposed to the 800-foot pattern flown by the other trainers. This allowed the pilot additional time for the numerous tasks and to compensate for the higher speed of the Harvard.

One early student, Jack Bolter, received a final briefing from his instructor before his first solo in the AT-6. The instructor, in the typical slow southern drawl, attempted to reassure an apprehensive Bolter, "Now see here Bolter, you're gonna find this here AT a bit faster and a bit more of a handful than that little old BT, so give yourself plenty of room. Go out a bit wider on your approach, for sure as hell, you're gonna be as busy as a cat covering up shit."[16]

Course 4 arrived in Terrell on September 25, 1941, and the school reached its full complement of 200 students.[17] Training involved all three types of aircraft, primary, basic, and advanced, and the sky around Terrell filled with trainers. These trainers fanned out over a rural landscape of small towns, forests, green pastures, and cotton fields interlaced with dirt roads and meandering creeks distinguished from the air by stands of trees left along the creek banks when the original fields were cleared.

Each day the flight schedule began when instructors with students slated for dual instruction, as well as solo students, walked from the trim white buildings with green roofs to the grass flight line and the rows of trainers. Dispatchers armed with clipboards and various official-looking papers scurried about calling out aircraft assignments. Moments later, as the engines turned over and started, blue-grey smoke poured from the exhausts of the blue and yellow primary and basic trainers and the silver advanced trainers. The trainers formed a line taxiing to the end of the takeoff area, and then the field reverberated to the sounds of engines advanced to full power as one by one the trainers took off for the designated practice areas. Primary students practiced to the southwest of Terrell and the basic and advanced students to the southeast.[18] The school designated a special triangular area fifteen miles northeast of Terrell between Wills Point and Quinlan to practice low-level flying.

As the planes took off, the remaining students boarded yellow school buses for the auxiliary fields. These buses rumbled down dusty roads and over wooden bridges accompanied by the students' laughter, group singing, and the frequent grinding of gears in the old transmissions. The songs ranged from sentimental to bawdy bordering on obscene. Frequently some member of the school staff on the bus would call for a song such as, "the one about cats on the roof."[19]

When the first session ended, the instructor and his first student landed at the auxiliary field and the second student climbed into the aircraft. The instructor and his last student flew back to the Terrell airfield at the end of the day. This routine increased efficiency and avoided congestion at the main field. The only problem arose when a thunderstorm or sudden change in the weather sent all of the trainers rushing back to the main field at the same time. Then the hastily improvised landing pattern became a drawn out melee of trainers jockeying for position. Surprisingly, accidents were extremely rare during these scrambles.

Even with the use of the auxiliary fields, the main Terrell airfield had begun to suffer from the continuous operations. The RAF officers' original concerns over the bare areas in the airfield created by the leveling and grading process proved to be well founded. One early student later remembered the Terrell field as "a dust bowl when dry and a glue pot when wet."[20] Plans to add oil stabilization to the field in early December 1941 failed to materialize.

Solo cross-country flights represented a maturing of the student who was no longer restricted to the practice area or the intimate scrutiny of his instructor. Confidence grew with the experience that came with ever-lengthening flights. One early student remembered his first cross-country flight from Terrell to Greenville to Wills Point and back to Terrell: "Had I known where to look, it would have probably been possible from about 2,000 feet to have seen all the way round the route without leaving the vicinity of the Terrell field."[21]

Ken Bickers of Course 4 took off on a solo cross-country flight to Commerce, Texas, sixty miles northeast of Terrell. Arriving approximately on time, Bickers circled the grass field, landed, and taxied up to the small airport building to have his log book signed as proof of the flight. Apparently the absence of any other Stearmans on the field did not trouble Bickers. On the porch of the building sat two grizzled old men. As Bickers approached and before he could speak, one of the men raised his hand and then with an air of disdain said, "Ah know—don't tell me, y'all British and y'all lost."[22] Bickers had landed at Sulphur Springs about the same distance from Terrell, but more easterly than Commerce.

Cadets quickly learned that virtually every Texas town had the name of the town painted on the water tower. Railroad tracks became known as the "iron compass" and the revolving, neon-outlined, flying red horse sign on top of the Magnolia Petroleum building in downtown Dallas provided a distinctive landmark at night.

Terrell residents visited the airfield frequently or parked along the northern boundary road to watch the aircraft. During the initial activity, one man called the base and asked for mufflers to be installed on the aircraft to eliminate the noise. A spokesman at the school replied that if that were possible, then bombing Germany would be considerably easier. A local woman called the newspaper office to complain about the noise from the airplanes flying over Terrell and demanded that something be done because she had developed "nervous strain." The patriotic (and unsympathetic) editor of the *Tribune* replied in print, "The strain might be a trifle greater if the planes were dropping bombs."[23]

British cadets arrived in Texas from a land ravaged by war and subjected to nightly blackouts and constant food shortages. Cadets marveled at the seemingly endless expanse of the Texas landscape, the brilliant lights of the cities, and the abundance of food.[24] Squadron Leader Mills, one of the early site inspectors for the new training program, remarked, "It's hard to become accustomed to so much space. We feel keenly that it is possible to put the whole of England and Scotland in this part of Texas—and still have space left over."[25]

Cadets were amazed by the sight of so many neon lights; everyone in Texas seemed to own an automobile (many of the British cadets had never even driven an automobile)[26] and someone had invented an outdoor theater "where you stay in your car!"[27] The young Englishmen had never seen anything quite like a jukebox and any number of eggs was available at breakfast. In England, eggs were rationed at one per person per week.

Ever mindful of Anglo-American relations, British officials gave each student destined for the United States a small blue book titled, "Notes for Your Guidance." The book began, "You are going to America as guests" and then explored various aspects of American life, defined the different geographical regions of the United States, recommended several books on American history, and offered tips on conduct. The small blue book described America as a "great, friendly, yet different nation" and warned students, "you will not be expected to tell your hosts and hostesses what is wrong, in your opinion, with them and their country." Students were also advised to be careful when asked about American aid to Britain, or to compare the relative merits of British and American aircraft. The book concluded by advising students to, "mingle freely with the people and partake generously of their natural hospitality."[28]

Although not covered in the blue book, British students were also warned to stay clear of one other subject—racial segregation. The majority of cadets found segregation distasteful and many felt the attitude of southern whites who professed to be religious, yet supported a segregated society, to be hypocritical. The effects of segregation were a daily reality.

Just after the school opened in August 1941, the local paper sponsored a cooking class held in the Terrell city auditorium. The recipes presented included a ham baked in Coca-Cola and a "national defense pot roast." The sponsors reserved a section of the auditorium balcony for "colored women" who wished to attend. Blacks were expected to step off of the sidewalk and into the street in order to allow whites to pass.

On his first visit to Dallas, cadet Paul Ballance boarded a bus and sat down toward the rear. An elderly white man in the front of the bus got up, came back and took Ballance by the arm and escorted him gently but firmly to the front of the bus. "You from England?" the man asked. After Ballance's confirmation, the man explained that the rear areas of buses were occupied by "nigras."[29]

As in most southern towns, the railroad in Terrell formed a visible boundary between races. Whites lived in the northern section of town while blacks populated the south side from the railroad tracks to the airfield. Cadets were advised not to venture off Adeline Street, which led from the field into town. There is no record of any incidents between the British students and the local black population; in fact most cadets remember the local blacks as typically smiling and friendly.

Ken Stott of Course 18 recalled conditions in Terrell: "It was very hot even in October, but the barracks were well ventilated. It was sheer luxury after the camps in Britain and Canada and all the barracks cleaning etc., was done by Negro workers. We were rather shocked at first at the way the Negroes were treated, but we had been warned by the RAF before we came to Texas not to engage in any argument regarding the Negro question in the Southern States. I don't think Negroes were allowed in town apart from Fridays which was allocated to them for shopping. They lived in a sort of shanty town between Terrell and the camp, and we sometimes had to walk through it to return to camp. It certainly opened our eyes."[30]

Local blacks were hired to work at the school as custodians or kitchen help. Cadets usually paid the young blacks hired to clean the barracks extra to spit shine shoes (a nickel) and make up the cadet's beds (fifty cents a week). Black workers at the base had a penchant for gambling and impromptu games of craps were common occurrences in a corner of the barracks or in the rear of one of the hangars.

One story may indicate either the condescending attitude of whites, or the true feelings of blacks concerning their social status. An instructor on his way to test-fly a Stearman asked a black custodian at the base if he wanted to go for a ride. "No suh" came the quick reply. "Why, Jim don't you want to be a pilot?" asked the instructor. Jim replied emphatically, "No suh, it's hard enough just being a nigger."[31]

On September 20, 1941, representatives from the Terrell Aviation School and the RAF asked for the donation of a portion of the municipal cemetery for possible future use by the RAF training facility.[32] England, with its extensive history as a colonial empire, involvement in numerous foreign wars, and a small land area at home, had long ago decided that servicemen would be buried where they fell. The Oakland Memorial Park Association responded by setting aside a portion of the Oakland Memorial Cemetery for the RAF.

In the fall of 1941, automobile makers began advertising the 1942 models, little realizing they would be the last new cars for four years. The United States had embarked on an extensive rearmament program and the auto ads usually included patriotic references to the car makers' involvement in the national defense. In Terrell newspaper ads, Oldsmobile touted the smoothness of its Hydra-Matic drive, the power of its 110 horsepower, eight cylinder engines, and the fact that Oldsmobile made artillery shells and aircraft cannons for defense. Buick continued its popular valve-in-head, straight-eight engine and also built Pratt and Whitney aircraft engines. Chevrolet built trucks for the army.

Terrell residents read daily newspaper accounts of the fighting in Europe where the German invasion of the Soviet Union slowed with the early advent of winter after a string of unbroken victories over Soviet forces. The battle of the Atlantic generated intense coverage due to the recent involvement of United States naval units escorting merchant convoys in the western Atlantic and the first reports of American casualties. In the Far East, Japanese officials condemned statements made by Secretary of State Cordell Hull and accused the United States of hindering Japan's establishment of "A new order in East Asia."[33]

In an effort to generate public support for increased defense spending, the United States government released fairly accurate descriptions of military weapons. These descriptions, including silhouette drawings, appeared in the local paper under the heading "Know America's Planes" and included aircraft such as the North American P-51 Mustang, Grumman F4F Wildcat, Douglas A-20, and Martin PBM patrol bomber. Ironically, in less than two months, these same details would be heavily censored in the name of national security.[34]

By the end of September, the second aircraft hangar at Terrell had been completed. Parachutes hung in a tall loft at the southeast corner of the hangar to dry before being repacked. The Link trainer building became operational on November 3.[35] The Link building initially contained four trainers and later expanded to house six trainers. Radio technicians Howard Maxwell, Fred Brewer, and Henry Whiting installed the necessary crystals in the basic and advanced aircraft radios (the Stearmans did not have radios) and supervised installation of the control tower radio. Local citizens with short wave radios could listen to the aircraft and control tower on 3810 kilocycles.[36]

The completion of the control tower and the full operation of the radio-equipped basic and advanced trainers raised another question. Communications radios in the United States were licensed and controlled by the Federal Communications Control Board (FCCB), the predecessor of the Federal Communications Commission. The school staff assumed radio procedures used at Terrell would conform to United States standards. The RAF staff, how-

ever, requested the school use RAF phraseology and procedures.
The question went all the way to the FCCB, which granted an exception and allowed the radio procedures used at Terrell to conform to RAF standards.[37] The FCCB assigned the call sign KTAS to
the Terrell control tower.

The school hosted several inspections by groups as diverse as
local businessmen, a party of national news reporters from as far
away as Kansas City and Chicago, and various military delegations.[38]
On October 14, 1941, representatives of the RAF, including Air
Member for Training, Air Marshal A. G. R. Garrod, Group Captains Carnegie and Lord Douglas Hamilton, along with U.S. Army
Brigadier Generals G. E. Stratemeyer and C. L. Tinker, and a host
of lower-ranking officers inspected the school.[39] Upon entering
the base, the group passed the foundation of the recreation hall.
When they left several hours later the walls of the recreation hall
had been rough-framed and were standing. One member of the
inspection team looked at the rapid progress and commented, "If
we don't leave immediately, we'll have to inspect the recreation
hall, too."[40]

Interest in the British students remained high. The RAF officers
participated in the opening of an air show at the old Arlington Downs
racetrack. The cadets were guests of honor at the Tri-County Agricultural and Livestock Show. The school continued to receive invitations for cadets to attend private homes for dinner or on weekends.
Mrs. Lon Cartwright, president of the Terrell War Relief Society,
appointed Miss Eva Bond to chair a committee to see that each cadet received an invitation for Thanksgiving and Christmas dinner.[41]
The War Relief Society asked for donations for the new recreation
hall. Donations, including a piano, a radio, books, records, and
musical instruments, came from as far away as Dallas.[42]

Volunteers from the Terrell Junior Chamber of Commerce took
one hundred cadets to the Majestic theater in downtown Dallas to
see the opening of the movie *A Yank in the RAF* staring Tyrone
Power and Betty Grable and also arranged for one hundred Southern Methodist University coeds to attend.[43] The cadets found the

Hollywood plot somewhat contrived, but enjoyed the movie's combat film footage and actual scenes of RAF bases in England.

While Terrell introduced the RAF to Texas-style livestock shows, softball games, and cook-outs, the RAF cadets introduced Terrell residents to dances such as the Palais Glide and the Lambeth Walk.[44] The cadets also formed two soccer teams, the Hurricanes and Whirlwinds (named after two RAF aircraft), which joined the Dallas soccer league. The Hurricanes won the prestigious Times Herald Cup as league champions in March 1942.[45] The Whirlwinds won the trophy the next year.

The British students at first seemed shy and reserved, but underneath the cadets had a propensity for group singing (almost unheard of among Americans) and a dry sense of humor. It was a rare student who was confident enough or rash enough to attempt humor with the lofty flight instructors, but others were fair game. Arriving for a navigation class, L. C. J. "Bonzo" Brodrick of Course 4 spoke up: "Morning Mr. Mabry sir. Got a new story for you today." R. E. Mabry, the navigation instructor, replied with a resigned air, "Let's have it then, Brodrick, ah guess ah'm going to hear it anyway." Brodrick with only a trace of a smile continued, "Do you know the difference between the Eskimos at the North Pole and Eskimos at the South Pole?" Mabry replied, "Ah guess I don't, so what is it?" Brodrick answered trying to feign a heavy Texas accent, "The Eskimos at the North Pole say 'uh uh' but Eskimos at the South Pole say 'uh uh, y'all.'" Smiles and scattered snickers from the class were usually met with stony silence from Mr. Mabry.[46]

On October 10, 1941, cadets under the direction of Flight Lieutenant Palmer staged a musical performance at the First Baptist church.[47] The well-received performance, titled "Hands Across the Sea" and sponsored by the Terrell War Relief Society, featured songs accompanied by cadets on the piano, violin, and organ. Contribution plates were passed to raise money for musical instruments. Following the performance, the ladies of the War Relief Society hosted a tea for the RAF officers and cadets. Performances such as this would be repeated throughout the duration of the school.

Along with the intense public attention shown to the cadets, the RAF staff attempted to balance the priority of training with public relations. Ever mindful of the value of favorable public opinion, especially in a neutral United States, the RAF staff attempted to accommodate various requests from news publications. In the early fall of 1941, *Look Magazine* approached the school with an idea for a feature story on No.1 BFTS.

The story line (totally fictional) concerned two RAF cadets (to be selected by the school, but they should be "good looking and have good teeth and broad shoulders") who see a picture of two Houston coeds and "enter into a lively correspondence." The two coeds arrange to come to Dallas and are met at Love Field by the RAF cadets (preferably in an "Army vehicle" which would provide "local color") who then give the girls a tour of the base, where they would be photographed "wandering around." That evening the two cadets take the two coeds to an "elegant restaurant in Dallas" and then back to Love Field so they can fly home before classes on Wednesday.[48]

Luckey referred the letter to Beveridge without comment. Even for an officer determined to bend over backward to promote favorable public relations and accommodate the news media, this farfetched proposal was too much. The straitlaced Beveridge found it incomprehensible that two RAF cadets would have time to correspond with two coeds, much less take time off on a training day to go to Dallas and pick up girls to show around the base, and in a military vehicle supposedly using lend-lease gasoline. He found it equally incredible that anyone would believe RAF cadets "are paid sufficient to entertain girls in a swank dive and dance spot in Dallas." Beveridge had no intention of asking permission for this scheme and concluded, "The whole idea is fantastically inappropriate to the fighting service of a nation at war."[49] Apparently *Look Magazine* took the story line elsewhere.[50]

Course 1 completed flight training on October 30, 1941. Of the fifty original cadets, thirty-six graduated. This twenty-eight percent failure rate compared favorably with both RAF and army flight training of the period.[51] The first course graduated with the minimum 150 hours of flight time. As efficiency increased, later courses reached the goal of 180 hours before graduation, until the training syllabus expanded. In recognition of their achievement, the cadets, along with the RAF officers and school officials, attended a dinner party at the Adolphus Hotel in Dallas.

The official summary of Course 1 found that training suffered from equipment shortages, lack of suitable maps and publications, lack of blacked out night flying experience, inclement weather, disruptions caused by the move, and not being able to fly over "European type land." The American instructors lacked "the uniformity of method of C.F.S. (Central Flying School) trained instructors." But, the report concluded, "A very satisfactory standard of flying has been achieved" and "The American instructors made up in enthusiasm and keenness what they lacked initially in knowledge of RAF methods."[52] The report also praised the high level of cooperation between the various stages of flight training in the BFTS system, which, the report noted, did not always exist in RAF flight schools.

The reference to "European type land" stemmed from the general opinion among RAF officers that navigation in the United States did not adequately prepare pilots for flying in Europe. Cities in the United States were farther apart, more distinctive, and therefore easier to locate. The United States generally offered better visibility and farmland in certain areas of the country was laid off in one-mile-square grids oriented north and south. European cities were more numerous, closer together, and had fewer unique traits. This fact, as well as an abundance of closely spaced rivers and railroads, made navigation in Europe considerably more difficult than navigation in the United States, according to the RAF.

In 1941, RAF pilots were either noncommissioned officers (sergeant pilots and warrant officers) or commissioned officers.[53] Even though contemporary sources mention that approximately one-third of flight school graduates were usually commissioned as pilot officers (the same rank as a U.S. Army 2nd lieutenant or a U.S.

Navy ensign) and the remaining two-thirds graduated as sergeant pilots, in actual practice the ratio varied considerably between courses at Terrell.

Early in the war, commissions were still influenced by the British class system. Students from good public schools and prominent families were more likely to be commissioned as officers than the sons of shopkeepers, regardless of flying ability. As the war progressed, however, the necessity for highly trained personnel, especially in teams such as bomber crews, eroded the class system and exerted a democratizing influence on British society.

Since the cadets of Course 1 had been individually selected for the new program, the RAF staff at Terrell recommended that twenty-three cadets (sixty-four percent) of this class receive commissions. Beveridge noted in the recommendation that the cadets had been specially chosen, "And it seems obvious that if by that fact they are to lose a chance of commissioning which they might have had had they not been chosen, a grave injustice will be done them."[54]

When the graduates of Course 1 left Terrell, local citizens gathered at the train station to say goodbye. Many presented the cadets with small presents. The tradition of Terrell citizens meeting each new course as it arrived and bidding farewell to each departing course remained throughout the operation of the school.

In the following months Palmer attempted to keep track of the first graduates of No.1 BFTS to determine the effectiveness of the training received at Terrell. His unofficial correspondence with Operational Training Units and other commands revealed several deficiencies which had already been noted, but virtually all later British commands commented favorably on the Terrell graduates' "general discipline, bearing and keenness," and felt products of the BFTS were "outstandingly above the average produced by the other training schemes."[55]

Full flight operations, including night flying and longer cross-country flights, brought incidents and mishaps. Trainers were dropped in from too great a height on landing and occasionally ground looped. As long as the control stick remained back and the propeller did not strike the ground, a ground loop usually resulted in nothing more than bruised ego and possibly minor damage to the wing tip. Misuse of brakes after landing caused several trainers to stand on their noses, or in rare incidents, to go all the way over on their backs. One instructor and his student escaped safely after their trainer caught fire after landing.[56]

A student became lost, ran out of fuel, and landed his BT-13 in a farmer's field near Edgewood, twenty-two miles east of Terrell. Luckey commented, "We are going to have a school in map reading very soon."[57] A student landed his Stearman on top of another Stearman waiting to take off. Both planes were destroyed, but the students emerged unhurt.[58] One student suffered minor bruises when he ground looped his BT-13 at Gray Field in Denison, Texas. Mechanics from the school traveled to Denison, disassembled the Vultee and trucked it back to Terrell for repairs. Instructor A. U. Stahl and his student B. P. Norwood bailed out of their PT-18 when the engine quit at night.[59] Both were uninjured.

Instructor S. A. Williams and his student, Leonard Stead, however, were seriously injured when their AT-6 overshot the landing area and crashed into a heavy road grader.[60] The operator of the road grader jumped to safety just before the impact. Both the instructor and the student were hospitalized in the Holton-Johnson clinic, but recovered fully. After his release from the hospital, Stead convalesced in the local home of Reverend and Mrs. Benjamin Bean, whose only son had been killed in a civilian flying accident.

Chief flight instructor E. Van Lloyd and his student escaped serious injury when their AT-6 failed to clear the trees at the north end of the field during a night takeoff. The Harvard plowed through the tops of the trees, sheared off one wing, took off a portion of the roof of a house beyond the trees, and came to rest in the garden behind the house. A woman, Maggie Frazier, her daughter Corrine, four-year-old grandson, and another five-year-old child, asleep in the house at the time, awoke amidst the debris, shaken, but otherwise uninjured. Frazier credited faith in the Bible for their deliverance.[61] The next day Terrell residents clogged the airport road to view the damage.

For almost six months the school had been fortunate. Except for the two serious injuries and several destroyed aircraft, the mishaps had been minor. That ended on the night of November 30, 1941, when Richard Mollett of Course 2 (one of the cadets held back from Course 1) took off for a night cross-country flight to Waxahachie, Texas, in an AT-6. The Harvard crashed just after takeoff several miles south of the airport and burned. Mollett became the first fatality at No.1 BFTS. He died only two days before graduation. Just before the crash, Mollett had radioed his takeoff time and the tower responded with a corrected time. Even though the exact cause of the crash will never be known with certainty, officials speculated that Mollett became distracted by the radio call and the demands of a night takeoff in the sophisticated advanced trainer.[62]

New rules were published which postponed the student's initial radio contact until three minutes after takeoff.[63] This interval allowed the pilot sufficient time to retract the landing gear (which required resetting the trim), set the engine and propeller controls (manifold pressure and pitch), switch to the right fuel tank (then work the hand operated wobble pump three or four strokes to ensure proper fuel flow), and stabilize the aircraft at the proper airspeed and climb attitude, before communicating with the tower.

The RAF officers, cadets, and school faculty attended the first military funeral in the RAF section of the Oakland Memorial Cemetery. The Anderson Clayton funeral home in Terrell handled the arrangements. A simple grey granite headstone, inscribed with the RAF crest, Mollett's name, rank, service number, and date of death, a Christian cross, and an epitaph selected by the family, marks the grave. The epitaph reads:

and so he passed over,
a valiant young heart
his spirit lives on.

One week after Mollett died, the world changed forever.

1. *Terrell Daily Tribune*, September 5, 1941.

2. Toward the end of the war several ground school classrooms were air-conditioned.

3. Officially the Vultee BT-13 Valiant, the trainer became known (not always affectionately) as the Vultee Vibrator.

4. Vultee later became a division of Consolidated Aircraft. Surprisingly, for an aircraft which never achieved widespread popularity, Consolidated and Vultee constructed 11,537 Valiants between 1939 and the summer of 1944 when production ceased. *Jane's Fighting Aircraft of WW II*, 219.

5. James, *Teacher Wore A Parachute*, 63.

6. Largent, *RAF Wings Over Florida*, 66.

7. Bert Allam, letter to the author, January 12, 2000.

8. *Terrell Daily Tribune*, September 11, 1941.

9. "Basic-Advanced Course Single Engine Syllabus (10 Weeks) For Use at British Flying Training Schools in U.S.A." Manual located in ORB.

10. When Peter Townsend, a famous RAF fighter squadron commander during the Battle of Britain, became a fighter pilot in 1934 he was told, "Only fools and owls fly by night." Townsend, *Duel of Eagles*, 168.

11. "Basic-Advanced Course Single Engine Syllabus (10 Weeks) For Use at British Flying Training Schools in U.S.A." Manual located in ORB.

12. ORB, September 26, 1941. Each AT-6 cost the United States government between $21,600 and $29,000 depending on equipment and date of manufacture. In 1943 North American named the AT-6 the Texan. The British had originally named the trainer the Harvard. While technically United States property, the AT-6s used at Terrell are almost always referred to as Harvards in contemporary sources.

13. *Jane's Fighting Aircraft of WW II*, 251.

14. Notes on the Army Air Corps tests of the AT-6 are contained on page 176 of an attachment to ORB.

15. ORB, September 28, 1941. There seems to have been no standard for the delivery of aircraft to Terrell. Some aircraft came directly from the factory, others came from various army fields, and in various quantities. The last four of the initial PT-18s were delivered to Terrell from Sikeston, Missouri. ORB, August 23, 1941.

16. A. J. Allam, unpublished manuscript titled "Into the Wild Blue Yonder," 1979. In the possession of the author.

17. Even though ORB, 21, states that Course 4 arrived on September 27, the *Terrell Daily Tribune* reported Course 4 arrived on September 25. The ORB final course report on page 328, notes Course 4 began training on September 26.

18. Bill Brookover, interview, January 9, 2000.

19. The song about "cats on the roof" had many different verses and variations, and is largely unprintable. U.S. Army and Navy pilots sang the same song and one version had vivid verses on the sex life of the armadillo. Samuel Hynes, *Flights of Passage*, 125.

20. Bert Allam, letter to the author, November 30, 1999.

21. Bert Allam, "Terrell Tales No.4," published in the No.1 BFTS Association newsletter.

22. Ibid.

23. *Terrell Daily Tribune*, August 28, 1941.

24. *Dallas Morning News*, June 7, 1941.

25. Ibid., May 31, 1941.

26. "Pilots for Britain," *Time*, November 10, 1941, 56.

27. *Dallas Morning News*, December 10, 1941.

28. Steward, "As the English See Us," 24-25, 96.

29. Paul Ballance, letter to the author, January 19, 1994.

30. Guinn, compilation of student recollections.

31. Slightly different versions of this story are found in several sources including *Detached Flight*, Volume III.

32. *Terrell Daily Tribune*, September 20, 1941.

33. This is not intended to be a detailed history of World War II, but is indicative of the articles in the local newspaper, which subscribed to the major international news wire services.

34. *Terrell Daily Tribune*, December 23, 1941.

35. ORB, November 3, 1941.

36. *Terrell Daily Tribune*, August 20, 1941, October 16, 1941.

37. ORB, September 12, 1941.

38. *Terrell Daily Tribune*, September 16, 1941.

39. ORB, October 14, 1941.

40. *Terrell Daily Tribune*, October 14, 1941.

41. Ibid., December 6, 1941.

42. Ibid., November 14, 1941.

43. Ibid., October 3, 1941.

44. Ibid., November 18, 1941.

45. ORB, March 22, 1942.

46. Allam, "Into the Wild Blue Yonder."

47. *Terrell Daily Tribune*, October 11, 1941.

48. Letter dated September 19, 1941, from James A. Mundell of *Houston Post* on assignment for *Look Magazine* to Luckey, located in ORB.

49. Letter dated September 23, 1941, from Beveridge to Luckey, located in ORB.

50. An article in the July 24, 1942 issue of *Look* titled "The Truth About Our English Allies" by noted novelist C. S. Forester used several photographs of RAF cadets at various social functions in Terrell.

51. Contemporary sources usually mention a failure rate in U.S. military flight schools of between thirty-three and forty-five percent. A *Time* magazine article in the November 10, 1941, issue mentions a forty-fifty percent wash-out rate in Arnold Scheme schools. A review of Major Long's thirteen Army primary classes at Love Field before the move to Brady, Texas, reveals a forty-two percent wash-out rate. "History of the Dallas Aviation School," Maxwell.

52. ORB, November 2, 1941.

53. In the United States services, almost all pilots were commissioned officers. The Army Air Corps and Navy had non-commissioned enlisted pilots in the 1920s and 1930s and a few still flew in World War II. The U.S. Army Ground Forces also had enlisted liaison and artillery spotter pilots.

54. ORB, October 28, 1941, 154.

55. Ibid., November 2, 1941. This report was written some sixteen months later and included the results of Flight Lieutenant Palmer's unofficial inquiries.

56. *Terrell Daily Tribune*, November 14, 1941.

57. Ibid., September 13, 1941.

58. Ibid., November 29, 1941. The student in the landing Stearman was washed out.

59. *Terrell Daily Tribune*, October 11, 1941.

60. ORB, October 2, 1941.

61. *Terrell Daily Tribune*, November 30, 1941.

62. ORB, November 30, 1941.

63. Ibid.

On Sunday morning, December 7, 1941, the Empire of Japan attacked Pearl Harbor and the United States entered the war. The next day aircraft at the Terrell school sat idle as groups gathered to listen to the latest details of the attack and discuss the monumental events. Some buffoon, seemingly always present in any gathering of men during times of stress, boasted, "We'll lick the goddamn Japs in sixty days." Others asked what the cadets thought. With typical British reserve, the cadets tactfully suggested that it might take a bit longer than that.[1]

The declaration of war immediately affected Terrell and the school. Guards were added at the front gate and the previously easy access to the base became restricted. Two days after Pearl Harbor the Terrell city marshal, Zeb Henry, arrested an "alien suspect."[2] Terrell merchants removed all merchandise made in Japan from store shelves. County commissioners passed an ordinance prohibiting parking on the airport road. A week after Pearl Harbor, Mrs. R. B. Wood of Terrell had still not received word of her son, Van Wood, and stepson, D. C. Ayres, both stationed on the battleship *Arizona*.

The Terrell city commission added an armed guard at the municipal water works and water employees were authorized to carry weapons.[3] Other cities across the United States took similar precautions because of a common fear of possible sabotage to municipal water supplies.

The Civil Aeronautics Authority suspended all private pilots' licenses pending a review of birth certificates, positive identification, and the administration of a loyalty oath.[4] Since the personnel at Terrell were civilians, this order grounded all of the instructors. A week later, at least eight instructors were still waiting for copies of birth certificates.[5]

Doctor and Mrs. W. A. Grant of Terrell were notified their only son had been killed at Clark Field in the Philippines on the first day of the war.[6] This was one of the first notices in what became a long list of casualties from Terrell and Kaufman County during the next four years. Just before Christmas, more than two weeks after Pearl Harbor, Mrs. Wood received word that her son and stepson had both been killed on the *Arizona.*[7] A week later Mrs. Wood suffered a near fatal heart attack. About the same time, Mr. and Mrs. Will Howard learned their two sons, also stationed at Pearl Harbor, were both safe.[8]

The office of Civil Defense took out full-page newspaper ads advising citizens on the proper procedures in case of an air raid. Governor Coke Stevenson added Terrell to the list of cities to receive an aircraft spotting station.[9] Local citizens signed up for courses in civil defense or first aid, while others volunteered to be air raid wardens. Two months after Pearl Harbor, Civil Defense authorities shipped 10,481 gas masks to Terrell, along with 200 steel helmets for air raid wardens, 40 pairs of firemen's hip boots, and 24 folding canvas cots.[10] The Iris theater added equipment so the movie could be interrupted for President Roosevelt's radio broadcasts.[11]

After Pearl Harbor the British cadets discarded the grey civilian suits and wore their blue RAF uniforms into town. The cadets were guests in Terrell and Dallas homes for Thanksgiving and Christmas.[12] Two cadets, H. A. Booth and D. Hutt of Course 4, received a free weekend Christmas flight to Kansas City and Chicago from Braniff Airways. The pair stayed at the Stevens Hotel in Chicago, attended a hockey game, toured the city, and gave numerous press interviews before returning to Terrell on Monday to resume flight training.[13]

After the holidays Beveridge wrote an open letter to the citizens of Terrell to express:

> Our gratitude and appreciation for the kindness and hospitality shown by people in Terrell and the neighborhood to our pupils over the Thanksgiving and Christmas periods.

In Britain, as in America, Christmas is the Festival of the Home, and it has meant a very great deal to our pupils so far from their own homes to have the opportunity of participating in your Christmas festivities. They came back to barracks, laden with gifts and eatables and one and all spoke of the good time they had.

May I add the thanks of the R.A.F. staff here to their thanks for a Christmas which could have been bettered only by one spent at home.[14]

Cadets continued to marvel at the large kitchens in local homes and the abundance of food.[15] Cadets noted a lack of good English tea, but were quickly introduced to iced tea and many cadets developed a fondness for the drink, especially in the Texas heat. Others compared the first taste of Coca-Cola to "brown shoe polish."[16] Some foods such as chicken fried steak and corn on the cob presented a new experience (corn was only used for animal feed in England). One cadet when asked to describe corn on the cob replied, "Well it was cylindrical with little things pasted all over it and it was yellow."[17] Grits is a term used in England to describe a mixture of sand and gravel. When cadets first heard the term used in connection with breakfast, they marveled that Texans consumed road surfacing material.

But these linguistic misunderstandings worked both ways. Many cadets, after an excellent dinner or weekend visit, referred to the lady of the house as very homely. The strange look in return must have confused the cadet. In England the term homely is used to describe a particularly neat and efficient housekeeper and is considered a compliment. More than one shopkeeper in Terrell used the friendly valediction, "y'all come back now" to a departing British cadet only to see the cadet turn around and reenter the store to see what the shopkeeper wanted.

In late December 1941, the RAF amended the flight training syllabus. Faced with the conflicting requirements for better-trained pilots and a finite and dwindling source of manpower, the RAF reached several decisions.

Tremendous strides in aircraft development had been made in the previous decade. Operational fighters such as the latest models of the Supermarine Spitfire and the new Hawker Typhoon, approached or exceeded speeds of 400 miles per hour. The new long-range four-engine heavy bombers, the Avro Lancaster and the Handley Page Halifax, were entering service.

To meet the demands of these sophisticated aircraft, the RAF raised pilot training requirements from 150 hours to 200 hours. Elementary training (primary in the American schools) rose from 70 hours to 91 hours. Advanced training (a combination of basic and advanced in the American schools) rose from 80 hours to 109 hours. In the BFTS program, course lengths increased from twenty weeks to twenty-eight weeks, with new courses scheduled to arrive at seven-week intervals. The revised program consisted of twenty-six weeks of flight training and two weeks of leave. The RAF proposed that the extra week of leave occur at the end of training, but the No.1 BFTS officers recommended the additional week of leave occur between basic and advanced. Time in the Link trainer increased from twenty hours to thirty hours.[18]

The RAF also instituted a change originally recommended by the RAF staff in Dallas following the incident of the two cadets in Course 2 who, after traveling from England to Texas, found they did not like flying. Others in the RAF had also recommended some form of familiarization flight for students before traveling to the United States. To help reduce the failure rate and the wastage associated with transporting cadets who washed out back to Canada for reassignment, all cadets destined for the American schools, after November 1, 1941, were given ten to fifteen hours of flying instruction in England at an Elementary Flying Training School (EFTS).[19]

The Air Ministry also decided that the new four-engine, long-range bombers would have only one pilot.[20] Another crew member, the flight engineer, would be trained to aid the pilot in routine flight matters and in case of an emergency. In a nation faced with a severe shortage of manpower, this decision considerably eased the demand for future pilots. Almost ironically, the decision tightened the requirements for flight students. The RAF notified schools and training commands to wash out those students who had not soloed in ten and one-half hours. Holdovers, except for illness, were discontinued and for the first time ground school failures were to be eliminated.[21] Considerably more leeway had previously been allowed local commands in working with individual students.

Students who washed out were sent back to Canada for reassignment. Most were sent to training bases to become bomb-aimers, navigators, wireless operators, or aerial gunners. Washing out could be psychologically hard on a student and most left Terrell with a heavy heart. Kenneth Stott of Course 18 washed out after twelve and one-half hours because of poor landings and the fact he could not seem to judge height on the landing approach. "After elimination, I was very depressed. At nineteen the world seemed to be at an end! I was not alone, as within a week a further eight had joined me. I had a Selection Board which consisted of the RAF Wing Commander and a Flight Lieutenant who were sympathetic and asked me my preference for another aircrew category. I said I wanted to be an air gunner, but looking at my record from ITW where I came second in navigation, they persuaded me to take a navigation course back in Canada, to which I agreed."[22]

In the years between the wars, both the military and civilian flight schools had worked to develop better training programs. These efforts resulted in improved training syllabuses, but little had been done to develop the profession of instructing. Most authorities still believed that a good pilot would naturally be a good instructor. Even the Army Air Corps, noted for its demanding standards for instructors, stressed flying "the Army way," with its emphasis on precision maneuvers. The RAF came close to understanding the proper role of the instructor when it noted, "The potential instructor must obviously be a keen and sound pilot who can persevere, and be patient and restrained under the tedium of long hours of repetitive work."[23]

The civilian flight instructors at the Terrell school had no common economic, educational, or social background. They came in all physical descriptions; some were quiet and soft-spoken, while others were gregarious, or even flamboyant. Away from the flight line the instructors were a diverse lot who represented the complete spectrum of American society of the time. Many of the instructors were married and led lives devoted to their families. Many drank only socially or not at all. Other instructors, however, engaged in endless partying, hard drinking, womanizing, and could be accurately described as exhibiting the lowest moral standards. The common thread that bound the instructors was a passionate love of flying.

The instructors at Terrell, although almost always good pilots, varied considerably as instructors. Bert Allam, an early cadet, is probably representative in describing his instructors. Allam credits much of his later success as a pilot to Bill Brookover, his primary instructor. Brookover combined patience with a genuine desire to see his students succeed. Allam's basic instructor, on the other hand, proved to be silent and uncommunicative, combined with a quick temper, and little patience. Allam even took the unusual step of requesting a change in instructor, which the school denied. Allam's advanced instructor, J. L. Isabel, proved to be entirely different from either of his earlier instructors. Isabel, a small man with a fierce reputation, could be critical and demanding, but Allam always found the instructor to be fair.[24]

Instructing required a fine blend of demonstration and observation. The student had to perform each maneuver or the exercise was meaningless. Instructors quickly developed a keen sense of self-preservation. One day Ray Flenniken, a newly promoted advanced instructor, returned to the Terrell field with a new student. As the Harvard touched down, it immediately swerved into a violent ground loop. The ground loop came so suddenly Flenniken could do nothing but hang on. The Harvard came to rest in the grass enveloped in a cloud of dust, but otherwise undamaged. Sitting in the Harvard with the engine idling and the dust settling, Flenniken, a conscientious instructor who did not believe in berating or intimidating a student, keyed the microphone and calmly said, "Now that wasn't a very good landing." But this time the student had the last word when he replied innocently, "Sir, I thought you were flying it."[25]

If nothing else, the Terrell instructors were highly individualistic. Cadet Don Stebbings and his primary instructor Bill Stewart, described as a "bronzed and lanky Old Gold smoking Texan," departed one day on an early dual cross-country flight. After takeoff, Stebbings got out his chart and notes, not realizing that Stewart had little use for formalized flight plans and believed in a more fundamental style of flying. Stewart suddenly rolled the Stearman inverted and Stebbings watched his chart and notes disappear below. Stebbings somehow completed the flight successfully and later described Stewart as "The greatest and indisputably the most colorful of all the instructors with whom I flew."[26]

Another instructor, Joe Lievre, taught combat aerobatics. Lievre, a fifty-three-year-old native of France, had reportedly taught aerobatics to Major Long at Kelly Field in San Antonio during World War I. Terrell residents watched enthralled as Lievre performed early morning aerobatic routines, which lasted up to forty-five minutes, high over the town.[27]

At the beginning of 1942, five instructors had been dismissed from the Terrell school as unsatisfactory.[28] Later in the year, in one of the more bizarre incidents, a student, Mead Barker of Course 10, returned to Terrell from a dual night cross-country flight from Terrell to Waco to Fort Worth, without his instructor. According to Barker, the instructor ordered an altitude of 5,000 feet after passing Waco and became upset when Barker replied that the flight plan for this leg of the flight called for an altitude of 7,000 feet. The instructor slammed the stick violently forward, then back, at which point the trainer stalled and entered a spin. Barker, at first thinking the instructor was still flying the AT-6, rode the aircraft down to 1,000 feet, and then managed to regain control. Realizing the instructor had bailed out, Barker flew the Harvard back to Terrell.

The instructor maintained Barker had been sightseeing and not paying attention to his altitude. The instructor claimed he had pushed the stick forward in order to make a point, not realizing he had removed his seat belt, and hit his head on the canopy. Dazed and finding the aircraft in a spin, the instructor bailed out. School officials believed Barker and dismissed the instructor.[29]

In the months following Pearl Harbor, the United States rushed headlong into the war effort. On the night of January 19, 1942, Terrell conducted its first blackout. For thirty minutes all lights in town were extinguished or covered, cars and trucks stopped, and the roads leading into town were closed. Under the direction of the city marshal, volunteer air raid wardens, assigned to various sections of the city, checked for compliance. An airplane from the school circled overhead and proclaimed the drill a complete success.[30]

Rationing of tires started in January 1942. New tires were available only after submitting a four-page "closely spaced" form.[31] The first month, Kaufman County received a quota of 149 truck tires, 50 passenger car tires, and 18 inner tubes. A Tarrant County preacher wrote to the state ration board and requested a waiver based on his calling and the Biblical admonition found in the Gospel of St. Mark, "Go ye therefore into all the world and preach the gospel to every creature." The unsympathetic, but Biblically literate, ration board wrote back denying the request and citing the Second Book of Samuel, "I will saddle me an ass that I may ride thereon."[32] At least four Terrell instructors purchased bicycles at the local White Auto Store.

In other areas, the government rationed sugar and a ban went into effect on rubber used in women's corsets, girdles, and other garments. The ban also included men's suspenders, garters, and elastic waistbands.[33] The army issued an urgent appeal for horses and mules and offered to pay $100 for light saddle horses, $165 for other horses, and $175 for mules. Due to a shortage of trained nurses American Airlines dropped its long-standing rule requiring flight hostesses to be registered nurses.[34] Citizens were told they should feel patriotic if their car engines knocked because fuel additives were now going to make the new 100-octane aviation fuels needed by warplanes.[35]

The Dallas minor league baseball club of the Texas League offered free seats to servicemen in uniform. The Terrell Aviation School asked if the offer included the RAF cadets. Team president George Schepps replied, "yes of course," but added, the offer did not apply to opening day, holidays, or playoff games.[36]

Against the backdrop of the new war excitement, the RAF cadets, under the direction of Flight Lieutenant Palmer, staged an elaborate New Year's show. The two-hour presentation in the Terrell High School auditorium included comedy skits, patriotic tunes, and the song "We're the boys of No.1 BFTS" written by Palmer (see Appendix C).[37] One of the cadet performers, Leonard Blower, had been a member of the British Broadcasting Corporation (BBC) chorus before the war. A *Dallas Morning News* reporter described Blower as "a British songbird."

The show ended with stirring renditions of "God Save the King," "There'll Always be an England," "The Eyes of Texas," and "The Star Spangled Banner" accompanied by the British and United States flags on stage. The RAF cast presented the well-received show again the next day in Terrell to another sell out crowd (admission twenty-five cents to go to the RAF recreation fund), the next day in Dallas at the Dallas Little Theater, and the next week in Kaufman.[38]

Newly arrived students received introductory lectures from the flight and administrative staff, which covered the training program at Terrell, ground school, examinations, proficiency checks, and the various rules and regulations. The cadets were reminded again that they were ambassadors for Britain, and in a lighter vein they were asked to remember that in America, squash is a vegetable not a game. Palmer usually concluded his address by stating that under no circumstance would any student drive an automobile while in the United States since "Americans drive on the wrong side of the road." Cadets were also advised not to go into a store and ask for a rubber: "The correct term in the United States is eraser."[39]

In spite of Palmer's rather dim view of driving in America, many of the British students did learn to drive while in Texas, and in time driving became quite a status symbol. Usually some member of a local family who had befriended a cadet gladly offered to teach the young man to drive. The ultimate prestige came when the British student drove the family to his own graduation ceremony and pulled into the base driving the family car.

As the world entered 1942, new courses arrived in Terrell as previous courses graduated and departed. By the middle of January, Course 6 had been training for almost six weeks, Course 7 was due to arrive in Terrell the next week, and Course 3 prepared to graduate.

On the cold night of January 18, 1942, cadet W. L. Ibbs of Course 3 became lost on a cross-country flight near Cumby, Texas, forty miles northeast of Terrell, and crashed when he ran out of fuel. Ibbs died two days before graduation and is buried in the RAF section of the Oakland Memorial Cemetery.

The death of Ibbs indirectly led to an unfortunate rift between Beveridge and the publisher and the editor of the local newspaper. It is perhaps inevitable that servicemen engaged in a world war and members of a free press will disagree on coverage of the conflict. The RAF, the same as other services, wrestled with the question of press releases and at one time ordered BFTS officers to withhold all information on accidents and fatalities.[40] This official prohibition led to the publication of information from other sources and inevitable errors. In early 1942, the RAF reconsidered this policy and authorized local commanders to release short factual press releases concerning events, including fatal accidents.

The account of the Ibbs accident in the local newspaper (written before the new policy) contained several errors, such as attributing Ibbs to Course 4.[41] Rather than simply informing the local editor of the new official policy regarding press releases, Beveridge wrote and asked (somewhat brusquely) that in the future unauthorized sources not be used for news stories. The publisher of the *Terrell Daily Tribune*, Fred I. Massengil, pledged his full cooperation, but, while glad to hear of the new policy, also defended the editor, H. Galbraith, and the previous story. Massengil admitted to being somewhat miffed at the implication of shoddy journalism.

Rather than allow the matter to drop, Beveridge and Massengil exchanged several letters vindicating their respective positions. Beveridge overreacted when he accused the paper of having a personal grudge against him. Massengil replied, "How you arrived at that conclusion passeth all understanding."[42] Beveridge also accused the newspaper of endangering national security by printing Ibbs's graduation date. Of course any enemy agent interested in the Terrell training schedule would have had to do nothing more than sit at the train station and note each arriving and departing class.

This petty exchange fortunately resulted in no lasting harm. Beveridge and his wife remained in Terrell until 1944, took an active part in local activities, and formed many lasting friendships in the community.[43] Both Massengil and Galbraith of the *Tribune* remained steadfast supporters of the school and the RAF students until the school closed.

Since the school opened, cadets marveled at the Texas weather. Even though several late fall cold fronts had sent night-time temperatures into the thirties, the temperature on Christmas day 1941 reached eighty degrees. A week later, on New Year's Day, the high temperature stood at fifteen degrees and two days later, three inches of snow covered the base.[44] Maintenance workers were thankful for the overhead gas heaters installed in the two hangars.[45] Flying continued even though temperatures dropped to six degrees the first week in January. In April 1942, Terrell experienced 17.4 inches of rain and for one twenty-four-hour period, all roads and rail lines into town were closed by high water.[46] But all British cadets agreed on one thing: what Texans called fog was nothing compared to a good London fog.

To ease the Terrell housing shortage, several local businessmen formed the Terrell Defense Housing Corporation in March 1942 and constructed ten new homes on Damon Street in north Terrell.

The frame homes cost $3,350 each and qualified for special benefits offered by the Federal Housing Administration (FHA) for new construction in areas classified as defense areas. These benefits included priority for building materials and special qualifications that allowed a defense worker to buy a home with no money down and a twenty-year pay out.[47] The group later constructed twenty additional houses.

In a further effort to enhance school spirit, the school published a book, similar to a college yearbook, titled "Detached Flight." The book contained a brief message from the RAF commanding officer and the school director, as well as photographs of the instructors, ground personnel, cadets, and routine activities around the base. The school published the first "Detached Flight" in March 1942. The name originated from a feeling of remoteness felt by the RAF personnel assigned to the Terrell school.[48]

On April 16, 1942, Lord Halifax, British ambassador to the United States, and his wife arrived in Terrell.[49] The couple toured the base, ate lunch in the mess hall with the cadets, spoke in Terrell, and dedicated a small monument at the RAF plot in the Oakland Memorial Cemetery. On the steps of city hall, Lady Halifax received a bouquet of Texas bluebonnets from two Terrell children. Then, under the Stars and Stripes and the Union Jack, Lord Halifax offered grateful thanks to the people of Terrell for "The kindness they have expressed in word and deed to my countrymen in training here."[50] Local press representatives were impressed that the lanky six-foot five-inch ambassador and his wife carried their own trays in the mess hall.

While touring the flight line, Lady Halifax spoke to an American cadet. As a child, the cadet had contracted infantile paralysis (President Roosevelt had the same disease). When the war broke out, the young man had been rejected for military service. He wrote directly to President Roosevelt and received permission to join the RAF.[51] Lord and Lady Halifax then traveled to Dallas and received the keys to the city from Mayor Woodall Rodgers. At a dinner reception that evening, Lord Halifax repeated a statement made earlier to the RAF cadets in Terrell: "I take comfort in knowing that Great Britain has lost only one war, and that to a United States which now stands beside us. The conclusion should be obvious to the most thick-headed German."[52]

British cadets regularly performed at local events and in local churches. A chorus of cadets under Palmer's direction sang at the city-sponsored birthday celebration for President Roosevelt held at the Terrell city hall on January 30, 1942. Cadet P. S. Walkins, in a notable achievement, played the world champion chess master George Koltenoski to a draw in Dallas. The entire cadet body marched into Terrell on Easter Sunday 1942 to attend church services.

Cadet Leonard Blower, the singer who so impressed the *Dallas Morning News* reporter at the New Year's performance, and a lay preacher, preached the evening service at the Terrell Methodist church on January 11, 1942. Blower titled his sermon, "Jesus is All the World to Me."[53] Three weeks later, Blower's AT-6 collided in midair with another AT-6 flown by Raymond Berry. Both cadets were killed in the crash and are buried in the Oakland Memorial Cemetery. When Blower's voice, which had graced so many musicals and church services, had been stilled forever, the entire town of Terrell mourned.[54]

A month later, Blower's younger brother wrote to Mr. and Mrs. A. H. Boyd of Terrell:

> We in England were deeply shocked, as you indeed must be, to hear that my brother was called to a greater world. Mum and Dad are heartbroken. . . . I would like to write thanking you for everything you have done for him. Would you please convey to all his friends in America our sincere thanks for the very kind and Christ like hospitality, which has been handed to him by everyone who came into contact with him. It was an extremely sad ending to a great Christian career, and as his brother, might I add, to a great friend and companion.[55]

The year 1942 proved to be a deadly year for accidents (see Appendix A for a list of fatalities at No.1 BFTS). Nine cadets and one instructor were killed. In addition to Blower and Berry, cadets Allan Gadd and Thomas Travers were killed in another midair collision. Besides Ibbs, cadet Aubrey Atkins also died during night flying. Another student, Geoffrey Harris, died when he bailed out and struck the tail of the aircraft. James Craig's aircraft crashed after it struck the beacon light at the Wills Point CAA field, while he and two other cadets were buzzing the field. The other two cadets were washed out and sent to Moncton for disciplinary action for unauthorized low flying.[56] The other accident involved the first instructor fatality when T. O. Somerville and his student, George Hanson, were both killed in the crash of a PT-18. The official inquiry concluded that Somerville, who had not flown for ten days due to an illness, allowed Hanson to stall the aircraft while flying too low, possibly simulating a forced landing.[57] Witnesses, however, reported the aircraft experienced engine trouble just before it crashed. As in so many cases, the exact cause will never be known with certainty.[58]

In the night flying accident in which Atkins died, school officials discovered that Atkins had been allowed to fly three and one-half hours that night: an hour and one-half more than the maximum permissible time for night flying. The school dismissed both the instructor and the flight commander involved. Amended orders were published that reiterated the maximum night flying times and restricted cadets designated for night flying to the base after duty in order to rest before time to fly.[59]

As the midpoint of 1942 passed, the school restricted flying for two weeks during the installation of a new 3,000-foot, north-south concrete runway. After completion, the radio-equipped basic and advanced trainers used the new runway, while the Stearmans took off and landed on the grass next to the runway. The local War Relief Society continued to knit woolen sweaters and socks for shipment to England. Terrell residents contributed to scrap metal drives aided by organizations such as the Boy Scouts. The United States imposed a speed limit of forty miles per hour on highways and the B. F. Goodrich Company in Akron, Ohio, announced the first tubeless tire.

Since the inception of the school, women had worked in clerical positions, in the maintenance department sewing and installing the fabric coverings on the aircraft, and as parachute riggers. As men continued to enlist for the war effort, manpower shortages resulted. For the first time, women were recruited to be Link trainer operators, and to work in the control tower and the engine maintenance shop.

In 1943 Pauline Bond had just graduated from Baylor University. Teaching in public schools for eighty dollars per month did not seem appealing. Born and raised in Kaufman, Bond had met several of the RAF cadets at local social functions. One of these, Brian Smith, suggested she apply for a job as a Link trainer operator. After Smith explained the purpose of a Link trainer and the role of the operator, Bond applied. Harding Lawrence, the head of the department, hired Bond, but only after explaining in the strongest terms that she would not date any cadet. The Link operators graded cadets' instrument proficiency, a task too important to allow personal feelings to possibly interfere. Bond (now Pauline Baxter) later remarked, "We were very formal in those days, even though we were both twenty-one, I called him Mr. Lawrence and he called me Miss Bond."[60]

As the war progressed, both the control tower and the Link trainers would be staffed almost entirely by young women. The Link trainer operators wore skirts, long sleeve khaki shirts, and ties. Dress codes for the controllers in the tower, however, were relaxed to allow slacks since the control tower could only be accessed by a tall outside ladder.

With the new Allied war effort and the expanded flight syllabus, the RAF staff at the Terrell school also increased. Flt. Lt. E. J. L. Robb arrived in July 1942.[61] Robb, an experienced Wellington bomber navigator, assumed duties as the station navigation officer. The arrival of Robb partially offset an acute shortage of ground school instructors.

While flight instructors were considered well paid, ground school instructors were paid considerably less. Flight instructors started at around $350 per month and received raises based on length of service and promotions to basic or advanced instruction. An instructor with several years' seniority could earn $500 to $600 per month at a time when airline copilots made around $250 per month.

Ground school instructors, on the other hand, were paid $200 to $275 per month. In March 1942, four of the seven original ground school instructors, including the chief ground school instructor, left the school and joined Pan American Airways.[62] Within two months, two other instructors left the school. By May the RAF staff described the shortage of ground school instructors as "acute."[63] Even though the school attempted to fill these positions, the replacements were not always satisfactory. In addition to the initial ground school instructors who left the school, three of the replacement instructors were dismissed as unsatisfactory. Even Group Captain Carnegie in Washington expressed his concern to Major Long.[64]

By the early fall of 1942, Course 12 had arrived in Terrell. Surprisingly, the results from the grading schools introduced in England to give initial flight instruction to students destined for training overseas, proved to be mixed. Terrell courses did experience a continual lowering of the time required to solo. Cadets in Course 2 soloed in an average time of just over twelve hours, while cadets in Course 5 averaged just under nine hours. By the time Course 10 graduated, the average time to solo had fallen to five hours and fourteen minutes, which is the time logged in Terrell and does not include flight time in England.

While the time required to solo declined, as could be expected, the wash-out rate varied considerably between courses. Course 1, a specially selected course, experienced a twenty-eight percent failure rate. The failure rate declined to just over fifteen percent for Course 5 and Course 7, but other courses experienced unusually high failure rates. Course 9 had a wash-out rate of over fifty-one percent. In Courses 8, 10, and 12, more than forty percent of the cadets failed to complete flight training. The exact reason for the differences in failure rates is unclear, but the RAF staff did note differences between the various courses.

Course 2, a rather average course, scored the highest overall grade of any BFTS in the final Wings Examination.[65] Course 7, which had one of the lowest wash-out rates, did poorly on the final Wings Examination. The RAF staff laid much of the blame for the deficiency on the high turnover rate among ground school instructors. Course 7 also suffered from "below average discipline and morale" which improved as the class progressed.[66] Course 8 was found to be "below average in every respect."[67] The staff noted Course 9 "Is from the point of view of general tone and morale one of the poorest so far produced by this school."[68] Both Course 8 and Course 9 suffered from high wash-out rates.

The most extreme comments by the RAF staff involved Course 4. The final report noted, "This course composed of mainly ex-Army and ex-RAF defense personnel, is well below the average of previous courses in all respects. The standard of flying was below average, elimination rate high, flying discipline poor and keenness indifferent. In ground school this course is much the worst course we have had."[69] Earlier Beveridge had written, "They (Course 4) are a poorly educated, ill-disciplined rabble and are far below the standard we would prefer to have as aircrew cadets."[70]

Aside from these comments, Course 4 appears rather average. Of the fifty-two cadets who commenced training, thirty-two graduated, for a thirty-eight percent failure rate (including two fatalities). Not the best, but far from the worst, and in line with comparable army and navy elimination rates. The criticisms of Course 4 may stem more from the type of personnel in the course, than from true deficiencies. These ex-British Army and ex-RAF ground personnel, some of whom had served in France, at Dunkirk, and in Norway, undoubtedly did not respond to the normal cadet routine and discipline with the same blind obedience as raw recruits.

Occasionally the cadets of Course 4 assembled under the leadership of one of the corporals in the class. Amidst the shouting of orders, the cadets would march to the flight line (marching and formal parades were rare at this time), out of step and with considerable shuffling of feet, accompanied by some bawdy ditty from their army days. The formation halted in front of the flight line with more shuffling and noise. The corporal would then advance smartly to the flight commander, give an exaggerated British salute, and in a loud voice announce, "A flight ready for flying, Sir!" Personnel on the base, attracted by the sheer volume of noise and commotion, were amused by these antics—all except the RAF staff. Only six graduates of Course 4 received commissions.[71]

The RAF staff felt that part of the problem lay in the small RAF contingent, and the fact that students at the school "had little chance to absorb a true Service atmosphere."[72] As a partial solution, the staff prepared to implement a new system of cadet discipline. The new system of discipline, enacted in all BFTS schools, became part of other sweeping changes in the BFTS system. The RAF closed No.2 BFTS in Lancaster, California, in December 1942 and the U.S. Army took over the school. Beginning in November 1942, class sizes in the remaining schools increased from 200 cadets to 300 cadets in three courses of 100 cadets each.

The availability of aircraft at this time had also changed, and the army experienced a shortage of basic trainers, while it had a surplus of advanced trainers. The Army Air Forces Flying Training Command asked the British, who had never been completely satisfied with the basic phase of training, if they would return their Vultee BT-13s, which would be replaced with AT-6 Harvards. British officials in Washington reported to the Air Ministry, "this, of course, suited us admirably, and brings the BFTS even more into line with normal RAF ideas" (British flight training consisted of two phases, elementary and advanced).[73] Students would now transition directly to the AT-6 from the Stearman. The school's original allotment of 75 aircraft (35 Stearmans, 20 Vultees, and 20 Harvards) increased to 103 aircraft consisting of 39 Stearmans and 64 Harvards.[74]

These changes coincided with the arrival of Course 13 on November 12, 1942. To house the new students and the increased RAF staff, a third barracks and a British administration building were constructed, and the school expanded the Link trainer building to include ten trainers. No.1 BFTS also received a new commanding officer. On October 7, 1942, Wing Commander F. W. Moxham, the previous commanding officer of the short-lived No.7 BFTS in Sweetwater, Texas, replaced Wing Commander Hilton, who returned to Bomber Command.[75]

Faced with a continuing pilot shortage, the U.S. Army Air Forces (previously the Army Air Corps) asked the RAF if army cadets could be accommodated at BFTS schools. For the first time, American cadets were slated to train alongside British cadets at No.1 BFTS.

---

1. Allam, "Into the Wild Blue Yonder."

2. *Terrell Daily Tribune*, December 9, 1941.

3. Ibid., December 10, 1941.

4. Ibid., December 9, 1941.

5. Ibid., December 12, 1941.

6. Ibid., December 17, 1941.

7. Ibid., December 22, 1941.

8. Ibid., December 18, 1941.

9. Ibid., August 22, 1941, October 16, 1941. The aircraft spotting station, manned by volunteers over thirty-five years old, was located on the Weatherford Dairy.

10. Ibid., February 18, 1942.

11. Ibid., December 13, 1941.

12. ORB, December 26, 1941.

13. *Terrell Daily Tribune*, December 26, 1941.

14. Ibid., December 30, 1941.

15. *Dallas Morning News*, December 10, 1941.

16. Flt. Lt. M. W. Palmer, "Open Letter to a U/T Pilot," *RAF Journal*, September 1944.

17. *Terrell Centennial 1873-1973*, 82.

18. ORB, December 27, 1941, December 30, 1941, and January 3, 1942.

19. Ibid., December 16, 1941, and letter from Group Captain Carnegie dated December 15, 1941, located on page 173 of an attachment to ORB.

20. Memorandum from RAF Delegation in Washington to all BFTS, located on page 351 of an attachment to ORB. In the United States services, blessed with an almost unlimited supply of manpower, multi-engine aircraft including twin engine transports and medium bombers were crewed by a pilot and copilot, both commissioned pilots.

21. ORB, May 26, 1942, 351.

22. Guinn, compilation of student recollections.

23. "A System of Elementary Flying Training," Air Ministry London, April 1941, located in ORB.

24. Bert Allam, letter to the author, January 12, 2000.

25. Ray Flenniken, interview by the author, Arlington, Texas, April 28, 2000.

26. Don Stebbings, "Terrell Tales No.36," published in the No.1 BFTS Association newsletter.

27. *Terrell Daily Tribune,* June 3, 1942.

28. Note contained in the Course 1 final report located in ORB.

29. Letter dated 18 December 1942 from Wing Commander F. W. Moxham to Group Captain Hogan located in ORB, appendix "A," 434.

30. *Terrell Daily Tribune,* January 20, 1941.

31. Ibid., January 9, 1942.

32. Ibid., March 11, 1942.

33. Ibid., February 27, 1942.

34. Ibid., February 25, 1942.

35. Ibid., February 12, 1942.

36. Ibid., February 25, 1942.

37. Ibid., January 2, 1941. ORB, January 2, 3, 4, and 9, 1941.

38. A slightly revised show was presented again the next year in January 1943. ORB and *Terrell Daily Tribune,* January 18, 1943.

39. Don Stebbings, letter to the author, November 8, 1993.

40. ORB, January 18, 1942.

41. *Terrell Daily Tribune,* January 19, 1942.

42. ORB Appendix, 191-97.

43. Beveridge's son Terry, born in Terrell, was named for the town.

44. *Terrell Daily Tribune,* January 3, 1942.

45. Ibid., November 6, 1941.

46. Ibid., April 21, 1942.

47. Ibid., March 6, 1942.

48. Six volumes of "Detached Flight" were published. Although published throughout the duration of the school, these six volumes did not cover every course. The Terrell Library has volumes III through VI. Volumes I and II are in the Terrell Heritage Society, and in Maxwell, microfilm roll A2281.

49. Even though Lord Halifax proved to be an excellent ambassador to the United States, many in Great Britain still resent his appeasement policies toward Germany during the years leading up to World War II. This attitude continued into the first year of the war when Halifax favored some form of negotiation with Hitler. For an analysis of the relationship and differences between Churchill and Halifax during the crucial period following the fall of France see John Lukacs, *Five Days in London: May 1940* (New Haven: Yale University Press, 1999).

50. *Terrell Daily Tribune*, April 17, 1942.

51. A photo of this meeting appeared in both *The Dallas Morning News* and *Terrell Daily Tribune* on April 17, 1942, without identifying the cadet. Bill Brookover, a former instructor, identified the cadet as R. R. Knowlton of Course 8, while Bert Allam identified the cadet as R. M. Baechle of Course 7. As many as ten Americans may have joined the RAF and trained at Terrell. The surviving official records are unclear on this point.

52. *Terrell Daily Tribune*, April 16, 1942, and April 17, 1942.

53. Ibid. January 10, 1942.

54. Guinn, "BFTS No.1 the Influence of Events."

55. *Terrell Daily Tribune*, March 2, 1942.

56. The final disposition of disciplinary cases sent to Moncton is unclear. In another case of a student washed out for leading an unauthorized formation flight that resulted in a fatal accident, rumors reached Terrell several months later that the student graduated in Canada and became an instructor. ORB, February 7, 1942.

57. Course 5 Primary Report dated January 27, 1942, located in ORB.

58. Only British cadets are buried in the RAF section of Terrell's Oakland Memorial Cemetery. Somerville's body was returned to his hometown of Berea, West Virginia.

59. ORB, February 14, 1942.

60. Pauline (Bond) Baxter, interview by the author, Kaufman, Texas, August 17, 2000.

61. ORB, July 20, 1942.

62. Ibid., March 1, 1942.

63. Ibid., May 8, 1942.

64. Letter from Carnegie to Long dated May 15, 1942, located in ORB, 350.

65. *Terrell Daily Tribune*, December 6, 1941.

66. ORB, Course 7 Final Report, appendix B, 372.

67. Ibid., 381.

68. Ibid., 420.

69. Ibid., 328, Course 4 Final Report.

70. Allam, "Into the Wild Blue Yonder."

71. Ibid.

72. ORB, Attachment, 421.

73. "Bulletin to Air Ministry from RAF Delegation Washington for Fortnight Ending October 17th 1942." Located in AIR 20/1387.

74. There is considerable correspondence from army officers in the Army Air Forces Flying Training Command concerning the correct allocation of aircraft for BFTS schools. Several officers felt the final allocation was excessive by army standards. This correspondence is located in Maxwell, microfilm roll A2281.

75. *Terrell Daily Tribune,* October 8, 1942.

Dallas Aviation School 1930. The hangar is one of the original wooden hangars constructed by the Army in 1917. From the collections of the Texas/Dallas History and Archives Division, Dallas Public Library.

Course 1, Dallas Love Field, June 1941. Note the news photographers in the foreground. From the No.1 BFTS Museum, Inc.

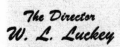

Major W. F. Long, operator (top) and L. H. Luckey, director (bottom), misidentified as W. L. Luckey, Terrell Aviation School. From the No.1 BFTS Museum, Inc.

Original RAF Officers, Wing Commander F. W. Hilton, chief flying instructor and commanding officer (top) and Squadron Leader A. Beveridge, chief ground instructor. From the No.1 BFTS Museum, Inc.

Flt. Lt. M. W. Palmer, first RAF administrative officer (top) and Flt. Lt. E. J. L. Robb, first station navigation officer (bottom). From the No.1 BFTS Museum, Inc.

School crest designed by cadet
Frank Miller, Course 1. From
the No.1 BFTS Museum, Inc.

E. Van Lloyd, Chief Advanced Flight
Instructor. From the No.1 BFTS
Museum, Inc.

Original control tower.
From the No.1 BFTS
Museum, Inc.

Link Trainer and operator. From the collection of the Terrell Heritage
Society

Primary Flight Line and Stearman Trainers. From the collection of the
Terrell Heritage Society

Course 4 class photograph. From the Margaret Bass photograph collection located in the Terrell Public Library.

Interior of the Bass Drug store, a favorite hang out in Terrell. From the Margaret Bass photograph collection located in the Terrell Public Library.

Ground school classroom. From the collection of the Terrell Heritage Society

Barracks (foreground) and British Administration Building. From the collection of the Terrell Heritage Society

Remains of the Harvard involved in the first fatal crash, November 30, 1941. From the Margaret Bass photograph collection located in the Terrell Public Library

Dedication of the RAF monument at the Oakland Memorial Cemetery by Lord and Lady Halifax, April 16, 1942. From the No.1 BFTS Museum, Inc.

Aerial view of the school taken from an AT-6; the new third hangar is at the top of the photograph. From the collection of the Terrell Heritage Society

Griffith auxiliary field operations building. From the No.1 BFTS Museum, Inc.

AT-6 Harvards in formation. From the collection of the Terrell Heritage Society

Ramp and flight line with the operations building in the center and the third hanger in the upper left of the photograph. From the collection of the Terrell Heritage Society

Gun camera image from a Harvard. From the collection of the Terrell Heritage Society

Wings parade and graduation ceremony. From the collection of the Terrell Heritage Society

Arthur Aaron, Course 6, awarded the Victoria Cross. From the No.1 BFTS Museum, Inc.

Course 21 prepares to leave Terrell, November 14, 1944. From the No.1 BFTS Museum, Inc.

Oakland Memorial Cemetery: "Some corner of a foreign field that is forever England." Photograph by the author

CHAPTER 6

EXPANSION

As the end of 1942 approached, the Allies took comfort in definite gains. Japanese expansion in the South Pacific toward Australia had been turned back in the Coral Sea. A month later, in June 1942, the Japanese navy suffered a crushing defeat at Midway Island, the turning point in the Pacific war, although few realized it at the time. In August, United States Marines landed on Guadalcanal in the Solomon Islands. Guadalcanal would be the beginning of the long road toward Japan itself.

In North Africa, the new commander of the British Eighth Army, Lt. Gen. Bernard Montgomery, decisively defeated the German Afrika Korps at El Alamein. At the other end of North Africa, United States troops landed in Morocco, while another force of American and British troops landed in Algeria. In November, Soviet troops surrounded the German Sixth Army at Stalingrad. As the brutal Russian winter descended, the plight of the 230,000 German troops became desperate.[1]

In spite of these gains, United States citizens and Terrell citizens were committed to a long and difficult struggle. The RAF cadets flew on Thanksgiving day and accepted no invitations to dinner.[2] In Terrell, the traditional Christmas ornaments along Moore Avenue were canceled as part of a national ban on outdoor decorations. Residents prepared for further rationing of items as diverse as canned goods, shoes, cheese, and meat. The government also banned sliced bread in an effort to conserve flour, but soon rescinded this rather dubious conservation measure. Gasoline rationing went into effect on December 1, 1942, amidst considerable opposition. Nonessential motorists received four gallons of gasoline per week.[3]

From the first halting, uncertain steps, the Allies had begun to forge a gigantic global war machine. Front line combat units were equipped and sustained by a vast and complex system of supply arteries that stretched across continents and reached back to individual factories and training centers. Huge bureaucracies sought to gain control over the production and allocation of war goods from raw materials, to tanks and aircraft, to toilet paper and toothpaste. No.1 BFTS in Terrell, Texas, lay at the very tip of this long and complex network of interlocking arteries supplying men and materiel to the Allied war effort.

No.1 BFTS started from the simple concept of utilizing an existing civilian flight school in Texas to train British pilots. As the Allied war effort gained global momentum, it reached out, embraced, and carried the Terrell Aviation School along with it.

The U.S. Army attempted to correct the early supply problems by adding a small contingent of army enlisted personnel to the Terrell school to coordinate supply needs. After the United States entered the war, the army assumed responsibility for the administration of the contract between the British government and the Terrell Aviation School under lend-lease.[4]

To ensure uniformity between the civilian contractors and to exert control over the administration of the various contract flight schools (more than sixty in all, not just the RAF schools) the United States government through the Defense Plant Corporation, a subsidiary of the Reconstruction Finance Corporation, purchased the physical assets of the school in June 1942. Major Long received $287,327 for the initial improvements, less any amounts still owed to the British government from advances. The six BFTS schools (which received consecutive PLANCOR numbers) retained their names and identities, but became the property of the U.S. government.[5]

By the summer of 1942, army training facilities had not been able to keep pace with the demand for pilots and the army asked the British RAF Delegation in Washington about the possibility of utilizing space in the BFTS schools. The RAF had already planned to expand the BFTS schools from 200 cadets to 300 cadets, and the decision to use only one pilot on the new heavy bombers had eased pilot requirements for the next six months. The RAF agreed to the army request and the intake ratio of the BFTS schools beginning with Course 13, set to arrive on November 12, 1942, became eighty-three RAF cadets and seventeen USAAF cadets.[6]

Before these plans could be implemented, though, the army reviewed the facilities at Terrell. The army found the Terrell medical arrangement to be woefully inadequate by army standards. The army authorized the construction of a new thirteen-bed hospital to be staffed by two army doctors and six enlisted male orderlies. The hospital would treat all emergencies and illnesses at the school. For any British cadet requiring hospitalization at any other army hospital, however, the British government would be charged $3.75 per day.[7] An ambulance, crash truck, fuel trucks, and additional ground transportation were also added at U.S. government expense.

Physical training facilities at the Terrell base were slated to be improved, along with the addition of an enlisted physical training instructor. The army reluctantly accepted the fact that the Terrell school had no swimming pool or gymnasium, both common on army posts. After several months of training, the army tested the Terrell municipal water supply and concluded that the water, although apparently good enough for Terrell citizens and the RAF staff and cadets, did not meet army standards. The city agreed to add more chlorine to the water.[8]

The army scrutinized even minor details. Obviously, British servicemen marched to different commands than their Allied counterparts. Army officials saw this as a potential problem and decreed that American cadets in BFTS schools would march in separate formations. The army quickly rescinded this absurd order and in the end, all cadets in BFTS schools were arranged in alphabetical order, without regard to service affiliation. At the school and individual course levels, British and American cadets lived together and trained together in complete harmony. The only area of friction, although it was always handled good-naturedly, concerned the matter of pay. British cadets received $25 per month, while army cadets were paid $75 per month.[9]

Since the civilian instructors were not part of a formal military unit, the individual schools prescribed loose dress codes. The instructors at Terrell usually wore leather flight jackets over khaki shirts and trousers along with a billed cap that resembled an airline pilot's or army officer's cap. The cap sported an emblem unique to the school with embroidered wings closely resembling RAF wings on either side of a shield with the words "No.1 BFTS." Concerned, the army training command in Fort Worth advised school officials in December 1942, "The wearing of any portion of the U.S. Army uniform or of Army insignia was in contravention of both Army regulations and the general law . . . . such uniform and insignia were worn at the peril of individuals concerned."[10] Apparently the school simply ignored this veiled threat.

The army also had concerns over the American cadets destined for training in BFTS schools. A memorandum dated December 8, 1942, to Colonel Price in Fort Worth stated:

> In connection with the BFTS schools, it is General Yount's desire that our Training Centers be informally advised, perhaps it could better be handled by telephone, to be very careful in the selection of American students to attend these schools. We have been somewhat critical in the past of British students. We do not want to leave ourselves open to any criticism from them. This information should be given to Training Centers unofficially and the British should not be aware of its existence.[11]

This concern resulted in the decision that all army cadets destined for training in BFTS schools would have prior flying experience. Army cadet L. G. Bue from St. Paul, Minnesota, who trained with Course 16 in Terrell, had a commercial pilot's license through the Civilian Pilot Training (CPT) program before joining the army. Ralph Breyfogle had been an instructor in the CPT program in

Akron, Ohio, and had 750 hours of flight time before joining the
army and training with Course 18 at No.1 BFTS. Even though Bue
and Breyfogle represented above average flight experience, most
army cadets who trained at Terrell had at least a private pilot's license.

Now that the army had responsibility for the school under lend-
lease, and army cadets were slated to train at Terrell, the army added
a liaison officer for training coordination, along with two enlisted
clerks to maintain records. Since the aircraft used at Terrell were
army property, the army also added an engineering officer and
several enlisted personnel as technical inspectors to ensure the
proper maintenance and inspection of the aircraft. All army personnel at Terrell were organized into a separate unit and designated the 321st Army Air Forces Flying Training Detachment
(AAFFTD).[12] At the inception of the unit in November 1942 (which
coincided with the arrival of the first American cadets) the supply
section continued to report to the Army Air Forces Supply Depot
at Randolph Field in San Antonio, but was later incorporated into
the 321st AAFFTD. In April 1944 the army redesignated the Terrell
detachment the 2564th Army Air Forces Base Unit.[13]

In anticipation of the increased size, the school entered into a
lease for 268 acres of the A. B. Griffith estate for a third auxiliary
field. The new field, located five miles west of the main airfield
and named Griffith Field, would be used by the expanded contingent of advanced trainers. The school constructed a frame building on the field, which housed a ready room, briefing room, and
two Link trainers so students could practice while waiting to fly.
The building also included a control tower. The Boykin auxiliary
field used by the primary trainers still had only a small frame shack,
a blackboard, and a water barrel. Students waiting to fly lounged
in the old school bus used for transportation or in the grass along
the field.

The increased size of the school caused a problem with the city
of Terrell. The original contract between the school and the city
called for the city to provide the school with free utilities (except

gas). Monthly utility expenses were already above original estimates and the city worried about the increased school size. In response to the city's concerns, Major Long agreed to pay all utility expenses over $500 per month (approximately half of the new utility expenses).[14]

The increased complement of advanced trainers included several equipped with gun cameras. Since the camera-equipped Harvards were limited, only about twenty-five percent of the cadets in the early expanded courses received an opportunity to view pictures taken during either simulated aerial combat or air to ground exercises.[15] In later courses all cadets were trained on Harvards equipped with gun cameras.

Both the army and RAF staffs included a physical training instructor. Physical training became a part of the school routine and included basic calisthenics, as well as skeet shooting, fencing, and archery. The two RAF soccer teams, now named the Spitfires and Hurricanes, won several additional trophies in the Dallas soccer league.

In addition to the new RAF commanding officer, Wing Commander Moxham, and the older staff members, Beveridge, Palmer, Robb, and Sergeant Moffat, the British staff now included two armament instructors, a station warrant officer, a second navigation officer, one signals NCO, and two enlisted administrative personnel. The growing British contingent and army personnel augmented the school's existing civilian staff.

As the number of cadets, RAF staff, army contingent, and the aircraft complement increased, the school's civilian staff also increased. The maintenance staff, under the supervision of Jimmy Hayden, the maintenance chief, and Jimmy Brown, the day supervisor, contained approximately forty workers. The maintenance staff performed all work on the aircraft except major structural repairs. Specialists worked on the aircraft engines, hydraulics, radios, and instruments, performed dope and fabric work, and periodically repacked the parachutes.

The civilian office staff included secretaries for the school, the RAF staff, and the army supply section. Due to the heavy accounting demanded by the various records, maintaining flight times, payrolls, invoices, and disbursements, the school employed accounting personnel, a full time auditor, A. L. Herberg, and a personnel director, W. E. Marshall. The school staff also included thirty kitchen workers, three in the canteen, fourteen in the Link trainer department, eight ground school instructors, and control tower operators, as well as custodians and janitors. This extensive staff supported the school's main purpose, which was carried out by thirty-five primary flight instructors and sixty-two advanced instructors (these numbers include supervisors and dispatchers).

Years later John McKenzie-Hall, an RAF gunnery officer assigned to No.1 BFTS, succinctly and accurately summed up the organization at the Terrell school. "I never fail to be amazed that such a hotch-potch of civilian and service personnel with all their different requirements and loyalties could work so well together in turning out a constant flow of very adequately trained aircrew."[16]

By the summer of 1943 various government bureaucracies vied for control over the nation's manpower supply. At the heart of this struggle lay the conflicting requirements for men for the various combat services versus the need for skilled war workers at home. When it appeared the priority of draft boards had been established, the army, fearful of losing trained personnel such as those employed at the Terrell school, came up with a novel solution. In July 1943, key workers at the school, such as flight instructors and maintenance personnel, were sworn into the inactive army reserve.[17] This action precluded the workers from being drafted, unless they left the school.

Throughout the physical expansion of the school the training routine continued. Each day swarms of trainers took off and fanned out over the surrounding landscape. The school continued to experience mishaps and accidents, but not all of the incidents resulted in injuries or fatalities. An early aviation sage once remarked that flying consisted of hours of boredom punctuated by moments of stark terror. This apt description also held true for learning to fly.

One morning in a clear fall sky an early basic student practiced aerobatics in a Vultee BT-13 in the training area southeast of Terrell. The mild temperature offered a welcome relief from the recent summer heat. After rolling out of a well-executed slow roll, the student's control stick remained hard over to the right. Unable to move the stick, the student began to panic as the BT-13 fell into a wallowing lazy spiral rapidly losing altitude. Application of full left rudder checked the spiral and with more power the student realized he could just maintain altitude. Now down to only 2,000 feet, the student had to decide quickly whether to bail out or remain with the aircraft, which was barely under control. He decided to stay with the plane and called Tarver field and asked that all other traffic be cleared from the landing pattern, which was immediately accomplished. The student made a wide skidding circular approach, descending by carefully adjusting the throttle. Now too low to bail out, the student realized he probably had only one chance at a landing, since it would be almost impossible to go around. The Vultee crossed the fence and dropped onto the grass. The sweat-soaked and still shaking student taxied to the flight line, shut down the engine and remained in the cockpit, silently contemplating the beautiful day and blue sky.

An instructor climbed onto the wing, slid back the rear canopy, and peered into the cockpit. In a matter-of-fact voice the instructor commented, "Oh nothing much wrong, just loose radio wires caught over the stick." The wires, which should have been securely clamped against the inside of the fuselage, had come loose and draped over the stick during the slow roll. The instructor unwrapped the wires and casually stuffed them into a recess of the cockpit. Later, the relieved student thought that the school, or the government, or someone should have shown a little more appreciation, or at least thanked him for saving the aircraft.[18]

Most students who progressed to the advanced stage of flight training began to feel for the first time that they might actually graduate. This realization, and the growing confidence which came from flying the AT-6, often led to overconfidence and a feeling of invincibility, a feeling that could be suddenly shaken.

More than one advanced student flying on a cross-country flight under a beautiful blue Texas sky sat serenely contemplating the passing scenery, his own quite considerable skill as a pilot, and his impending graduation, when the engine of the Harvard suddenly and without warning quit. Panic quickly followed the deafening silence. Fortunately, students had been drilled to immediately switch to the reserve fuel tank in case of an engine failure. Most engine failures resulted from fuel mismanagement, which meant the student failed to switch fuel tanks and simply ran one tank dry. The reserve tank was used for takeoffs, landings, and in the event of an engine failure. In virtually every case the engine roared back to life after a few seconds, and the humbled student continued the flight.

Even though the North Texas area experienced unusually heavy rainfall during the first eighteen months of the school's operation, Texas weather usually provided ideal flying conditions. But Texas weather, influenced by Pacific cold fronts and warm moist air from the Gulf of Mexico, could change quickly. As massive frontal systems battling for supremacy advanced and retreated across the landscape, the line of contact between the fronts resulted in low clouds, rain, or massive thunderstorms depending on the season.

Blue northers are particularly fast-moving cold fronts heralded by solid walls of dark blue menacing clouds. A blue norther in January 1943 resulted in a fifty-eight-degree drop in temperature during a twelve-hour period. March 1943 experienced three northers. The broiling summer sun routinely sent temperatures to near 100 degrees, thinning the air and decreasing aircraft performance. As the earth heated unevenly, flying at any altitude below 5,000 feet became uncomfortable due to rising thermals. High winds described by several witnesses as a tornado struck the base one June night in 1943, took off several roofs, overturned a storage building, and damaged several planes. Violent thunderstorms, many with large hail, were common during the spring and summer. On at least two occasions, the base experienced one of the strangest phenomena, a dust storm straight out of West Texas. On one of these occasions, two newly arrived British cadets were walking to the main gate when the wind rose, the sky rapidly turned crimson, and the sun grew dim. One cadet looked at the eerie sky and asked the guard, "Does this happen here often?"[19]

The RAF implemented the new system of cadet discipline with the arrival of Course 13 and the American cadets. This system divided each class into flights and appointed cadets to cadet officer and enlisted ranks to oversee the daily administration and discipline of the flights. The ranking cadet in the senior course held the rank of cadet wing commander. Cadet officers supervised daily activities such as reveille, working parades, color hoisting and lowering, reporting defaulters, punishment drills, lights out, and bed checks. Cadet officers also handled minor disciplinary matters and could impose limited punishments such as confinement to camp (CC) during open post on the two weekday evenings (Friday evening had been added to Wednesday evening as open post, subject to the flight schedule), polishing all boots in the barracks, scrubbing the barracks floor, and tours of extra drill.[20]

The RAF staff handled any serious breaches of discipline, which usually involved violations of flight rules such as unauthorized stunting or low flying. Violations of this nature normally resulted in elimination from the program, especially if the violation resulted in an accident. The only serious nonflying breach of discipline occurred in August 1944 when two cadets from Course 20, who had been policemen before the war, caught another cadet stealing money. The RAF ordered a military court martial and the accused cadet held in the Army stockade at Majors Field in Greenville, Texas, thirty miles north of Terrell. The court martial found the cadet guilty and he returned to Canada under guard.[21]

The new commanding officer, Wing Commander Moxham, instituted another change at No.1 BFTS. Up until this time, most (but not all) graduating classes attended a dinner in Dallas at the completion of training as the only acknowledgment of their achievement. After leaving Terrell, the new RAF pilots returning to England drew the coveted wings, the outward symbol of their status as rated pilots, at the supply depot in Moncton, New Brunswick. Raymond Stanley of Course 3, one of the courses that did not even have a farewell diner in Dallas, later recalled: "My last flight on the course was a night flight which ended in the very early hours of the morning. There was a light covering of snow on the ground and I finished the flight with a burst tail wheel tyre. After taxiing to the hangar, I was informed the course had ended. There was no graduation ceremony. A very few days later, we were paraded, bid goodbye and entrained for Moncton. I was now a qualified RAF pilot with the rank of Sergeant."[22]

Beginning with the graduation of Course 9 on November 10, 1942, the school held an elaborate Wings Parade and graduation ceremony. The ceremony commenced with a march past of all cadets followed by speeches and the presentation of wings to the individual graduates. Visitors, including local citizens, were invited to the ceremony along with dignitaries from the Army Air Forces Flying Training Command and the RAF Delegation in Washington.[23] An army band from either Majors Field in Greenville or the Waco Army Air Field played while the RAF flag flew from a mobile flagpole. Major Long presented an engraved silver cigarette case to the top graduate of each course.

Although individual American and British cadets lived and trained together in complete harmony, friction developed between some BFTS schools and their army contingent. The army officers assigned to BFTS schools as liaison officers were also rated pilots. Some of these Army Air Forces officers, especially in the Southeast Training Command, saw themselves as the commanding officers of the American cadets and felt that all matters involving the American cadets, especially washing out an American cadet, required their approval. Even though there is no evidence of friction at the Terrell school, considerable correspondence devoted to this subject originated in other areas.[24]

Major General Yount, commander of the Army Air Forces Flying Training Command, attempted to resolve the conflict by issuing a series of directives that clarified the role of the army officers assigned to RAF schools. The army officers were to act in a liaison capacity only and all decisions affecting the operation of the school (and any American cadets training in the schools) were the sole responsibility of the RAF commanding officer. Yount based his decision partly on the fact that British cadets trained in army schools under the Arnold Scheme had always been under the command of the local army base commander.

Even then the issue did not completely go away. Several months later, in response to inquiries concerning the applicability of army proficiency standards to army cadets in BFTS schools, General Yount wrote in another letter to all training commands, "It is desired to reiterate that the RAF commanding officer has complete charge of training and is responsible for establishing levels of proficiency."[25]

United States Army cadets trained at No.1 BFTS beginning with Course 13, which arrived in Terrell on November 12, 1942, through Course 19, which graduated on June 18, 1944, when the output of army training facilities began to exceed the demand for pilots. The army selection process for training at a BFTS often began with a notice on the bulletin board.

Ben Brown from Toledo, Ohio, joined the Army Air Forces after receiving a private pilot's license. One day in San Antonio while in preflight, the training phase before cadets entered flight school, Brown saw a notice on the bulletin board for anyone with flying experience interested in training at an RAF school. He thought the idea sounded like fun and shortly afterwards he and his boy-hood friend John Wilson were on a train bound for Terrell to join Course 18.[26]

A total of 138 American cadets trained with No.1 BFTS.[27] Army graduates of BFTS schools were authorized to wear both the silver Army Air Forces wings and RAF wings. Considering that the army only sent cadets with previous flying experience to BFTS schools, it is not surprising that the American cadets excelled at the flight program. An American cadet graduated as the top cadet in three of the seven courses that contained American cadets, even though

American cadets made up less than twenty percent of each course. It is somewhat surprising that the American cadets did not fare as well with ground school subjects. Even though the records are incomplete, at least fourteen American cadets at Terrell washed out from failing ground school.[28] This discrepancy almost certainly stems from the fact that British Initial Training Wings (ITW), which potential flight cadets attended for eight weeks before entering flight school, emphasized ground school subjects such as navigation, meteorology, and mathematics.

From the inception of the program, army cadets trained in BFTS schools were slated for either transport or ferry commands.[29] The reasons for this decision are unclear. Even though transport and ferry duties were essential to the war effort, the vast majority of cadets considered transports mundane and longed for the glamor of flying fighters. It is difficult to understand why the army made this decision before training even commenced, especially since those cadets selected for RAF schools had to have prior flying experience and could be expected to be among the best cadets.

Starting with Course 13 and the inclusion of American cadets, the RAF made a further modification to the training syllabus. Even though the Stearman was universally regarded as an excellent primary trainer, students gained little from the decision to extend the primary training phase to ninety-one hours. The real benefit of the expanded training syllabus came from the increased experience in the more sophisticated advanced trainer. While retaining the new total flight time of 200 hours, the RAF amended the primary phase of flight training back to the original 70 hours and extended the advanced stage to 130 hours.

Even though minor modifications were later made in individual categories, the training syllabus took the following format:[30]

Primary			
Dual:	General	22 hours
	Instrument	6 hours
	Day Navigation	3 hours

Night Navigation	1 hour	
Night Local	3 hours	
Total Primary Dual:		35 hours

Solo:	General	29 hours	
	Day Navigation	4 hours	
	Night Local	2 hours	
Total Primary Solo:			35 hours

Total Primary:		70 hours

Advanced:

Dual:	General	21 hours	
	Instrument	22 hours	
	Night Local	5 hours	
	Formation	4 hours	
	Day Navigation	7 hours	
	Night Navigation	5 hours	
	Armament	2 hours	
Total Advanced Dual:			66 hours

Solo:	General	17 hours	
	Night Local	7 hours	
	Formation	8 hours	
	Navigation	24 hours	
	Armament	8 hours	
Total Advanced Solo:			64 hours

Total Advanced:		130 hours

Total Primary and Advanced:	200 hours

In response to the shortage of ground school instructors, the school hired a new chief ground school instructor, J. G. Williams. By mid-1943, the shortage of ground school instructors had been largely alleviated. The increased RAF staff augmented the school staff and the school successfully hired additional qualified instructors. One of these, Marvin Krieger, had been an animator for several Hollywood studios including Columbia and Warner Brothers before the war and then a navigation and meteorology instructor at the short-lived No.7 BFTS in Sweetwater, Texas. When No.7 BFTS closed after the first primary class, the army converted Avenger Field to train the newly created Womens Airforce Service Pilots (WASPS). After teaching for several months at the new army airfield, Krieger came to Terrell in the fall of 1943.

Flying had been curtailed one day by a low solid overcast when a silver Lockheed P-38 Lightning appeared under the clouds and circled the field. The Lightning, a large, heavily armed, twin engine fighter, and one of the fastest fighters of World War II, generated considerable interest when the pilot reduced power and lowered the landing gear, obviously intent on landing. The P-38 made a perfect landing and taxied to the flight line where the pilot shut down the two 1,425-horsepower Allison engines as students and instructors crowded closer to get a look at the big fighter. They were surprised when the canopy opened and a petite, very good looking, young woman in her midtwenties emerged from the cockpit. Seeing Krieger, the young woman, one of his former students at Sweetwater, threw her arms around Krieger and gave him a big hug, much to the envy of everyone present. Krieger became the hero of the base.[31]

The increased number of cadets, the larger RAF staff, the new army detachment, and the necessary increase in instructors and maintenance personnel, required changes throughout the base. In addition to the new third barracks, hospital, and RAF administration building, the school also authorized the construction of a third hangar. The base layout now resembled a capital A, with the original administration building at the apex. The other buildings occupied the area between the apex and the cross bar. With the new hospital and the increased RAF and army staffs, the original dispensary in the recreation hall became the officer's mess. The two original hangars formed the right leg of the A and the new third hangar formed the left leg.

The original RAF officers had been correct when they insisted that Major Long include the recreation hall with the school facilities. The recreation hall, which featured interior walls finished in natural knotty pine and pictures of the King and Queen of England draped with a British flag above each entrance, became a favorite place to relax after hours.

At night the recreation hall filled with the voices of young men intermingled with popular tunes from the jukebox or radio. The radio stayed tuned to KRLD in Dallas or the sentimental favorite, KSKY, "Your station in the sky, situated on top of the beautiful Hotel Stoneleigh overlooking downtown Dallas." The jukebox played the big band sounds of Glenn Miller, Tommy Dorsey, Les Brown, Harry James, Benny Goodman, and Artie Shaw, such as "Sentimental Journey," "Chattanooga Choo Choo," "Night Train," and "Moonlight Serenade." Individual singers such as Bing Crosby and Dinah Shore were popular and the local girls were crazy about a skinny new singer named Frank Sinatra (even though many of the men couldn't understand why).[32] The silky smooth voice of Vera Lynn sang, "There'll be blue birds over the white cliffs of Dover. . . . there'll be love and laughter and peace ever after—tomorrow when the world is free. . . . just you wait and see." Many of the young men relaxing, chatting, writing letters, and listening to these songs would never live to see the end of the war.

The RAF staff, cadets, and the school's civilian staff were often asked to speak at various luncheons and organizations in both Dallas and Terrell. Wing Commander Moxham, a former Boy Scout in England, spoke to Dallas Boy Scouts. C. H. Siebenhausen, a flight commander, spoke to the local Rotary club on the future of aviation. Local civic clubs frequently hosted speakers from the school. RAF Cadet Jack Crook of Course 18, who held a master's degree from Konigsberg University in East Prussia, spoke to the Dallas high schools social studies club.

Parades and war bond drives in both Dallas and Terrell provided additional opportunities for participation by cadets and the school staff. At one war bond drive, Terrell residents had an opportunity to view the Japanese two-man midget submarine captured at Pearl Harbor. The seventy-nine-foot-long submarine toured the country loaded on a flat bed trailer.[33] Those who purchased war bonds could climb a wooden walkway and look into the submarine through holes cut in the hull and covered with plexiglass.

Early courses had marched in formation into Terrell for Easter church services. Church attendance now became a regular occurrence. The first Sunday morning of each month, Palmer led the cadets into town along tree lined streets to attend church services. Catholics attended Mass at 8:30 and Protestant services were held at 11:00.

One particularly beautiful Sunday morning Palmer noticed an unusually large group assembled for early Catholic Mass and correctly concluded that many of the cadets were anxious to start open post and meet friends in town or in Dallas. In a stern voice Palmer told the assembled cadets that to change one's religion in the RAF without the approval of an officer of at least the rank of Group Captain constituted a serious offence.[34]

While not flying or studying, cadets found many places to relax away from the school. Numerous residents of both Terrell and Dallas held perpetual open house for the cadets. Herbert Corley, the owner of McCords Department Store in Terrell, frequently took cadets home for supper. Mrs. S. J. Bass, the outgoing and flamboyant owner of the Bass Drug store, continuously welcomed and entertained cadets. The Bass Drug became a favorite hangout noted for its soda fountain, milk shakes, and malts. The United Service Organization (USO) opened canteens in Dallas and Terrell. These canteens provided a convenient place to sit and drink a soft drink, listen to music, or talk. The women of the Terrell War Relief Society hosted teas and dances. The American Legion regularly hosted dances. Other diverse organizations such as the Hockaday School and Junior College in Dallas and East Texas State Teachers College in Commerce, Texas, invited cadets to dances and parties. Local citizens installed a bench on Moore Avenue with a sign exhorting drivers to give a cadet a ride to Dallas. Cadets never waited long for a ride.

Strangers on the street regularly invited cadets to their homes for supper or weekend visits. One evening, Mrs. Cora Jackson received a call from her son. He had noticed a British cadet standing under a street light on a Terrell corner, alone and obviously homesick. He asked his mother if she could set another place for supper. The cadet, along with several other British cadets, joined the Jackson family. This hospitality was typical not only in the Jackson home, but in many other Terrell and Dallas homes as well.[35]

The RAF used the expanded advanced time for longer cross-country flights inaugurated by Course 13. In May 1943 Course 14 embarked on a two-day 1,600 mile cross-country. The route arched through West Texas, Kansas, Oklahoma, and Louisiana before returning to Terrell.[36] A large transparency with the outline of England, Ireland, Scotland, and northern Europe superimposed on an aeronautical chart of Texas and the surrounding states hung in the ready room. From this map, cross-country flights could be planned with Terrell in the same relative position as London. These long cross-country flights simulated flights to all countries surrounding Great Britain.[37]

After several dual and solo cross-country flights in the Harvard, including two low-level flights at 500 feet, advanced students were paired on the longer flights. On these long cross-country flights, one student flew while the other navigated. On the next leg of the flight, the roles reversed. The student navigator removed the control stick in the rear cockpit and used a board to spread out charts, flight plans, and instruments. Pilots on these long flights took devilish delight in waiting until the student in the rear seat was engaged in some particularly difficult navigation problem and then rolling the aircraft inverted or pushing the stick violently forward, inducing negative g's.

On the return leg of a cross-country flight to Shreveport, Louisiana, Alan Bramson of Course 16 pulled this stunt on his navigator, Bryan Baker, only to hear Baker snicker, "Well laugh that off." Bramson turned around to find Baker's leather helmet, goggles, and headset stuck in the broken plexiglass canopy. Bramson had slammed the stick forward not realizing Baker had removed his seat belt to retrieve a pencil. Baker hit the canopy with enough force to break the plexiglass. Bramson, the cadet wing commander and top cadet in the senior class, contemplated a dismal future in the infantry upon his return to Terrell.

After the Harvard landed, mechanics had to remove the jammed canopy in order to free Baker from the rear seat. Bramson assumed his best maligned countenance as he told the chief flight instructor about having to take sudden evasive action after being bounced out of the sun by an Army P-51 Mustang (a common enough practice among newly commissioned army fighter pilots). The chief flight instructor looked skeptical, but the barely plausible story obviously could not be confirmed by the fictional army pilot. Several days later Bramson graduated as the top cadet of Course 16. Bramson, a nonsmoker, left Terrell with the engraved silver cigarette case he received from Major Long.[38]

In June 1943 the base added a two-story operations building next to the flight line between the two original hangars and the new third hangar.[39] The operations building contained a supply room for flight gear, briefing rooms, offices, and a cadet ready room. The operations building also had a new glass-enclosed control tower on top of the building. The control tower operators no longer had to scale an outside ladder to reach the tower.

The last major improvements to the airfield included a new 3,000-foot northwest-southeast concrete crosswind runway and a concrete apron in front of the new operations building. The apron extended from the two original hangars across to the third hangar. The new runway and flight line were scheduled for installation in the fall of 1943, but revisions to the specifications, renegotiation of the contract, winter weather, and rains the following spring delayed construction until July 1944. Construction activity virtually suspended flight operations for several days.[40]

In June 1944, the army installed a weather station on the second floor of the operations building staffed by an officer and eight enlisted personnel.[41] The weather staff later expanded to three officers and nine enlisted men. The weather station was upgraded to a Type A weather station several months later, and the staff began taking twenty-four-hour weather observations. The weather station, however, came too late to prevent the worst tragedy at No.1 BFTS.

On the cold morning of February 20, 1943, a flight of nineteen Harvards with thirty-eight cadets from Course 12 took off for a low-level cross-country flight to No.3 BFTS in Miami, Oklahoma. A grey misty overcast obscured the sky, but the sketchy weather forecast predicted improving conditions. Several of the school staff, including Jane Howell, a Link trainer operator and former meteorology and navigation instructor, watched with an ominous sense of foreboding as the planes took off.[42]

As the day progressed, the weather continued to worsen and the school issued a recall to the aircraft now approaching the rising terrain of the Kiamichi mountains in southeastern Oklahoma. Fourteen of the Harvards returned to Terrell. Two planes that did not hear the recall message reached Miami. The other three planes were missing.

In one of the planes, pilot John Wall and navigator Gordon Wright found themselves trapped in a valley surrounded by heavily wooded hills which extended upward into the dark grey overcast. Noticing a small clearing, Wall pulled the power, banked the Harvard steeply to remain within the narrow confines of the valley, lowered the landing gear and flaps, and made a perfect precautionary landing.

After calling the Terrell school, Wall and Wright (nicknamed "Wilbur" Wright) were advised to remain with the plane until the weather cleared. A young couple, Mr. and Mrs. E. F. Jordan who lived next to the field, took the two cadets into their home. After supper Wall and Wright decided that duty required them to guard the Harvard. Wright drew the first watch, while Wall retired to bed. A short time later Wall heard a gentle tapping on the first floor bedroom window. Raising the window, he found Wright thoroughly soaked by cold rain and sleet, which had begun to fall. The two cadets conferred again and decided the Harvard would probably be safe from Axis saboteurs. Wright crawled through the window and both cadets climbed into the large bed beneath mounds of blankets.

The next day Wall and Wright joined searchers from nearby communities and parties that had arrived from the school in Terrell to search for the two missing planes. That afternoon searchers found one of the missing Harvards and recovered the bodies of Vincent Cockman and Frank Fostic. The following day searchers found the other Harvard along with the bodies of Michael Hosier and Maurice Jensen. Both Harvards had crashed into the mountains obscured by haze and thick low clouds.[43]

Ten personnel died in accidents in 1943. In addition to the four cadets killed in Oklahoma, cadet M. W. A. Williamson, army cadet Howard Perry, and instructor Cliffard Levan were killed in a mid-air collision. Cadet Kenneth Coaster ran out of fuel near Waxahachie, landed in a field and called the school. His instructor M. B. McDonald brought fuel to the site, but both the student and the instructor were killed on takeoff when the Stearman failed to clear the trees at the end of the field.[44] Cadet Alan Langston landed at Terrell after a night flight and inadvertently taxied into a stock tank left over from the field's agricultural past. The aircraft overturned and Langston drowned before help could arrive.[45]

Amazingly, there were no fatal accidents in 1944.

---

1. Messenger, *The Chronological Atlas of World War Two* (New York: Macmillan, 1989), 104-5, 112-13, 118-19, 126-27.

2. *Terrell Daily Tribune*, November 26, 1942.

3. Ibid. December 1, 1942.

4. Maxwell, microfilm roll A2281, frames 348 and 349.

5. Guinn, "BFTS No.1 the Influence of Events." Also see a report titled, "Synopsis of Engineer's Final Report of Defense Plant Corporation, an Instrumentality of U.S. Government, PLANCOR 1483, Terrell Aviation School Limited, Terrell, Texas, August 1, 1944." Located in the National Archives, Record Group R6 234, Selected Records Box 527, Plancor 1482 and 1483. This report contains a complete inventory of the physical assets of the Terrell school, and a short history of its acquisition. The report refers to many of the school buildings as, "constructed prior to 1941." No school buildings were constructed before 1941. Apparently the notation should have read, "constructed prior to December 7, 1941."

6. In actual practice the number of American cadets in courses 13 through 19 (the courses with both American and British cadets) varied slightly from course to course.

7. Maxwell, memo dated January 4, 1943, contained on microfilm roll A2281, frame P0552.

8. *Terrell Daily Tribune,* July 8, 1943.

9. The difference in pay is mentioned in numerous later interviews and writings and applied to all British and American servicemen, not just flight students.

10. Contained in Maxwell, microfilm roll A2281, the statement is attributed to a Colonel Price. The RAF had given permission for the school to use the facsimile of RAF wings in the cap insignia.

11. The memorandum is signed simply "K.P. Mc." and is almost certainly from Colonel (later Brigadier General) Kenneth P. McNaughton on the staff of Major General (later Lieutenant General) Barton K. Yount, commander of United States Army Air Forces Flying Training Command. Located in Maxwell, microfilm roll A2281.

12. Maxwell, "History of the 321st AAFFTD." The 322nd AAFFTD was assigned to No.3 BFTS in Miami, Oklahoma, and the 323rd AAFFTD was assigned to No.6 BFTS in Ponca City, Oklahoma.

13. The Terrell Army detachments were commanded by Captains D. R. Longino, B. F. Baker, E. W. Zwicker, J. W. Rees, and R. F. Grunert.

14. *Terrell Daily Tribune,* January 20, 1943.

15. Maxwell, "History of the 321st AAFFTD," 8.

16. Guinn, "BFTS No.1 The Influence of Events" and compilation of student recollections.

17. *Terrell Daily Tribune,* July 13, 1943.

18. Allam, "Into the Wild Blue Yonder."

19. *Terrell Daily Tribune,* July 27, 1943.

20. ORB, November 15, 1942. Also, ORB appendix, 421-23.

21. ORB, August 14, 1944, has a list of the court officers, but this entry is strangely silent on the exact nature of the charges. Additional details of this incident were supplied by Alan Bramson in his letter of May 27, 2000, to the author, and from information provided by Joe Tymon, a former cadet in Course 20.

22. Guinn, compilation of student recollections.

23. Brig. Gen. T. W. Blackburn, commander of the 31st Army Air Forces Training Wing at Enid, Oklahoma, delivered the graduation address to Course 13, the first course to include both British and American cadets. Blackburn had been taught to fly in World War I by the RAF. *Terrell Daily Tribune,* May 25, 1943.

24. Copies of this extensive correspondence are located in, "History of the 321st Army Air Forces Flying Training Detachment, Terrell, Texas," Maxwell, microfilm roll A2281.

25. Letter dated December 29, 1943, located in Maxwell, microfilm roll A2281.

26. Ben Brown, phone interview by the author, February 12, 2000.

27. This number is a compilation of individual course reports found in ORB, confirmed by course photographs in the Margaret Bass photograph collection in the Terrell Public Library. The number includes ten Army Air Forces cadets who transferred from Ponca City, Oklahoma, when No.6 BFTS closed in April 1944. ORB, April 17, 1944, *Terrell Daily Tribune*, April 18, 1944.

28. Maxwell, "History of the 321st AAFFTD," 6. Army Air Forces cadets who failed the RAF ground school were allowed to complete flight training at an army facility.

29. Ibid., 5.

30. Located in ORB, and Maxwell, microfilm roll A2281.

31. Marvin Krieger, interview by the author, Dallas, Texas, February 21, 2000.

32. Allam, "Into the Wild Blue Yonder."

33. *Terrell Daily Tribune*, February 9, 1943. The Japanese midget submarine is now on permanent display at the Admiral Nimitz museum in Fredericksburg, Texas.

34. Ray England, "Terrell Tales" published in the No.1 BFTS Association newsletter.

35. *Terrell Centennial 1873-1973*, 82.

36. ORB, May 26, 1943.

37. Maxwell, "History of the 321st AAFFTD," 1. Pictures of the map appear in *Detached Flight* and the map is described in a May 1, 1944, *New York Times* article and in Wiener, *Two Hundred Thousand Flyers* (Washington: The Infantry Journal, 1945), 45-46.

38. Alan Bramson, letter to the author, July 29, 1994. Also *Terrell Daily Tribune*, December 6, 1943.

39. ORB, June 23, 1943.

40. *Terrell Daily Tribune*, October 11, 1943; ORB, July 1-4, 1944.

41. ORB, June 16, 1944.

42. Howell's husband, Garnett Howell, was an advanced flight instructor at the school.

43. "AT-6s Crash Near Moyers During WW II." Sixth grade reading project. Rattan, Oklahoma elementary school 1997-98 project, copy located in Terrell Public Library. Also *Terrell Daily Tribune*, February 22, 23, 24, 1943.

44. *Terrell Daily Tribune*, September 21, 1943. One report indicated that McDonald may have attempted to do a slow roll on take off, but no firm evidence exists.

45. *Terrell Daily Tribune*, February 2, 1943. Langston's parents were interned in Hong Kong by the Japanese.

By the late spring of 1944, the Allies had amassed huge numbers of men, aircraft, and ships, as well as vast quantities of equipment, supplies, and support facilities in England. It was no secret that this massive buildup heralded the invasion of Europe, the long-awaited and much-discussed second front. On the morning of June 6, Terrell residents heard the first radio reports of Allied landings in the Normandy area of northern France. Businesses in town closed for an hour and churches opened as Terrell residents prayed for the success of the invasion.[1]

The successful D-Day landings assured the outcome of the war, although much hard fighting and many casualties still lay ahead. At the Terrell school, Course 19, the last course to include American cadets, graduated on June 18, 1944.

With training commands now meeting the demand for pilots, the RAF raised the requirements for new pilots to 210 flight hours and shortly thereafter to 220 hours.[2] What had started as a twenty-week course of 150 flight hours during the early war years when England stood alone against the Axis powers, had evolved into a thirty-two-week course of 220 hours with Allied victory in sight.

The RAF had done much to alleviate the original feeling of remoteness felt by the personnel at Terrell. An RAF supply section at the school now stocked uniforms, shoes, and miscellaneous items. A library included general service information. From early 1943, combat veterans regularly visited Terrell to talk about operational lessons learned from combat experience. The staff noted, "Talks by ex-operational pilots are considered here to be of the greatest value to instructors and cadets alike, situated as this Unit is so far from actual operations."[3] Specialists, such as R. J. Hutchins of the Sperry Gyroscope Company, also visited the school to talk on various subjects. Hutchins lectured on the intricacies of gyro instruments.

Cadets continued to arrive in Terrell and depart from Terrell on a regular basis. The first, as well as the last sight of Terrell a cadet had was the train depot next to the Texas and Pacific railroad tracks. Terrell residents gathered at the stately red brick edifice, topped by a steep roof and two brick corner towers, to welcome each class and see each class off after graduation. Arriving cadets stepped off the train to be greeted by military officers from the school, local residents, and the sights and sounds of rural East Texas. Various freight sat piled next to the depot, cars and trucks passed in the distance, while wagons loaded with cotton or other farm goods pulled by mules and usually driven by black farm hands waited to be unloaded. Into this new experience the arriving cadets often heard the sound of aircraft engines and instinctively gazed upward to see Stearmans or the powerful Harvards flying low over the town as they entered or departed the airfield traffic pattern.

Only a few years before, these same young men now arriving in Terrell had been too young to join the service, but had thrilled to the stories of the RAF fighter pilots who turned back the German Luftwaffe during the Battle of Britain in the summer of 1940. Some who lived in southern England had watched the high weaving contrails in the cobalt blue sky as British Spitfires and Hurricanes clashed with German Messerschmitts, Heinkels, and Junkers. Those closer to the coast saw the aftermath as the dogfights descended and the German planes headed for home, usually just off the ground with low fuel warning lights already on, often pursued by British fighters. Many times they saw the results of these clashes.

Eric Gill, a teenager living near the English Channel, and his friends were the first to the scene of several crashes. The boys amassed a small collection of souvenirs from the wrecks. One day the local constable arrived at Gill's house and spoke to his father. It seems the government wanted back the complete .303-caliber

Browning machine gun Gill found near the wreckage of a Hurricane. As soon as he could, Gill joined the RAF and arrived in Terrell with Course 20.[4]

No matter how large the school became or how favorable the trend of the war news, the training of each new course remained much the same. Instructors guided and agonized over students, and each new group of cadets learned anew the lessons of flight. Cross-country flights continued to provide unusual experiences.

Two Terrell students, Ben Brown and Don Cross of Course 18, were on a long cross-country when Cross, who was flying the Harvard, became ill. As Cross felt worse the cadets conferred and decided to land. Cross picked out a long straight section of farm road "somewhere in Oklahoma or Arkansas" and managed to land, then staggered down from the front cockpit and became violently sick. Unable to continue flying, Cross climbed into the rear cockpit and Brown took off and flew to Shreveport, Louisiana. Cross, by then feeling much better, flew back to Terrell. No one noticed the switch.[5]

Arthur Ridge, a primary cadet in Course 25, became lost north of Dallas on his first cross-country flight and decided to land when his fuel ran low. Ridge landed in a farmer's field soft from recent rains and the Stearman bogged down. Looking for assistance, Ridge approached a nearby farmhouse and knocked on the door. A large, rather formidable-looking, black woman appeared complete with a red bandanna over her head. Ridge, whose total knowledge of southern racial norms probably came from the movie *Gone With the Wind* (the black woman even resembled Hattie McDaniel who played Mammy in the movie), straightened to his full five-foot seven-inch height and asked politely, "Is the master at home?" The woman stepped back and slammed the door without a word.

Ridge then gave a farmhand a dollar to hitch his mule to the landing gear of the Stearman. When the mule failed to make any progress, a new idea occurred to Ridge. He started the Stearman's engine in order to aid the effort. The noise, however, only terrified the mule. The animal bolted forward, the reins slipped up the landing gear and were promptly cut by the propeller, which dumped the mule unceremoniously on his nose in the mud. The offended mule took off in full flight toward the next county. Ridge finally succeeded in extricating the Stearman, determined his location, and returned to Terrell.[6]

Even advanced students were not immune from the learning process. Instructor Ray Flenniken and his student took off from El Paso, Texas, on a flight to Albuquerque, New Mexico, the next leg of a long cross-country. The student made a flawless climbing turn to altitude and leveled off, but on a southerly heading. Flenniken sat quietly for a few moments as the Harvard flew unerringly toward Mexico, then keyed the microphone and calmly asked, "Are you sure this is the way to Albuquerque?" The head in the front cockpit went down, followed by a shuffling of papers, charts, and flight plans. The student's head reappeared and the Harvard turned to a new course, almost the exact opposite of the previous course. "Sorry sir, I was using my ground speed for the heading."[7]

The periodic proficiency checks could also provide unexpected experiences. Cadets approached these flights with some apprehension since even a minor mistake could result in elimination from flight training and an uncertain future. Frank Jones of Course 17 flew his final check ride with E. Van Lloyd, the chief flight instructor. Part way through the flight Jones flew the Harvard through a graceful slow roll. At the top of the roll, the Harvard's rear cockpit waste tank, installed for the relief of pilots on long flights, opened and the odoriferous contents drenched Van Lloyd. Jones quailed as Van Lloyd ordered him to immediately return to the airfield. After landing, Van Lloyd paused just long enough to say to Jones, "Not your fault," before striding explosively toward the hangars and the maintenance crew that should have drained or at least secured the waste tank.[8] Jones breathed a sigh of relief.

Despite official prohibitions, many young men learning to fly sophisticated military aircraft, regardless of nationality or service affiliation, could not resist the urge to show off. Flying low and fast provided a thrill that all too often resulted in tragedy. Common targets were farmhouses, cars on roads, and the ultimate allure of

flying under a bridge. At least two Terrell cadets flew through telephone wires or low power lines while buzzing the ground and still
managed to stay in the air. Another cadet forced a Greyhound bus
off a road. Not long after the beginning of the war, army and navy
officials in North Texas asked citizens to report low-flying aircraft.

A week before the D-Day landings, representatives from two lo-
cals of the Southwestern Telephone Workers Union demanded the
Dallas City Council take action to curb low-flying and stunting aircraft over the city.[9] The union contended that the problem had
become so acute that third-shift war workers, who had to sleep
during the day, were being disturbed. The commanding officer of
the Dallas Naval Air Station feebly suggested that many of these
incidents came from military aircraft taking off or landing at local
airfields. But the problem of low flying was real enough.

The secret to not getting caught buzzing, according to Ben
Brown, an American cadet with Course 18, was to never stay around
long enough to let someone on the ground get the aircraft number. The individual aircraft numbers were small and with military
training facilities located in Dallas, Fort Worth, Denton, Waco,
Greenville, Corsicana, and Bonham, besides Terrell, it was difficult
to determine which field a low-flying trainer came from.[10]

One night Ted Langston of Course 16 could not resist the urge
to fly around the red Pegasus sign on top of the Magnolia Petroleum building in downtown Dallas (the Magnolia building was the
tallest building in Dallas). After circling the sign at its level, Langston
leveled out only to be confronted in the darkness by the tall smoke
stacks of the Dallas municipal water works located on the northwest outskirts of town. Even if Langston exaggerated when he later
told of flying between the smoke stacks, dimly outlined against the
night sky, the sobering experience came close to being deadly.[11]

Even the young instructors at Terrell were not immune from an
occasional desire to show off. One day primary student Don Ashby
of Course 19 heard his instructor, J. W. Talley, a former crop duster,
say, "I've got it." Talley, obviously bored, then descended over one
of the county farm-to-market roads. At flying speed, the main wheels

touched down on the narrow road and the instructor held the stick forward to keep the tail in the air as the Stearman drove down the road. An old car appeared around a bend and confronted the aircraft head on. Talley held the Stearman on the pavement until the last moment and then eased back on the stick. The Stearman hopped over the car and then settled back onto the road. Ashby looked back to see the shaken farmer emerge from the car that was now resting at an angle in the ditch.[12]

Not all low flying came from showing off. One beautiful Monday morning, Ted Nieass, a primary cadet in Course 24, realized his slow rolls were less than precise, but he was startled by the string of oaths from his instructor, Nelson Grisham, in the front cockpit. Grisham, slowly recovering from a weekend of partying and not in the best humor, saw his favorite cigarette lighter fall from his pocket as the Stearman rolled inverted. Grisham took the controls, spiraled down and then proceeded to stand the Stearman on its side while he and Nieass inspected several acres of field with the wing tip "barely above tall grass level."[13] The search proved fruitless, which did nothing to improve Grisham's mood. In spite of this incident and frequent Monday morning hangovers, Nieass always regarded Grisham as an excellent instructor.[14]

Air Commodore H. E. Howell of the RAF Delegation in Washington delivered the graduation address to the cadets of Course 20 on August 25, 1944. Howell commented that the recent mixing of American and British cadets "had done more to promote and cement the friendship between the two great allied countries than would be accomplished in the field of diplomacy."[15] On a personal note, Howell reflected that he was too old to fight in the current war and asked the cadets to pay back the Germans for him. Howell's home in England had recently been destroyed by a German V-1 flying bomb.

One of the most enduring aspects of the story of No.1 BFTS is the strong and long-lasting relationship between the young British flight students and the people of Terrell and Dallas. This bond of friendship did not end when the cadets graduated and left Terrell, but continued during the war and long after the war.

Numerous families and individuals such as Una Pierce Kilpatrick of Dallas maintained a perpetual open house on weekends for the British cadets. The cadets, who helped in the kitchen and in her garden, came to regard Kilpatrick as a second mother. One former cadet later wrote, "When we left Texas last Monday we really knew how much it had meant to us. There wasn't a cheer as the train pulled out. Our hearts felt empty and it was a sorry day for us."[16]

Andrew Bayley of Course 17 remarked later:

> During our stay in Texas, the hospitality and friendship offered to us by citizens was little short of amazing. Dr. and Mrs. Guessner of Dallas afforded three fellow cadets and me generous hospitality and sleeping accommodation on Saturday nights when we could visit Dallas. They also fed us on Sundays and often we accompanied the doctor on his rounds on Sunday mornings. They attended our wings presentation, drove us back to Dallas and took us out for a meal and entertained us for the rest of that weekend. I shall never forget them![17]

In Terrell, Mrs. O. I. Cole, the hostess of the local USO, stayed in touch with many of the cadets she came to know. John J. T. Johnstone of Course 17 later wrote:

> I shall never forget the wonderful times we used to have, just chatting over a cup of tea or sitting around the piano singing the old songs. You know, you were more than just a hostess to the English fellows, for you filled the place of those ladies who were most dear to us, but were 7,000 miles away. I don't think you could ever know how grateful we and hundreds of mothers and fathers in England are to you.[18]

The strong ties evidenced by the British cadets remained throughout the operation of the school. Duncan Hancock of Course 27, the last course in Terrell, later reflected:

RAF cadets had been training in Texas since 1941 and yet by 1945, practically every weekend some 300 of us disappeared into Dallas or Terrell, the great majority to be guests of families in the towns. We were entertained royally, sometimes in wealthy households, but frequently by families of (by American standards) quite limited means. Two families with whom I stayed on numerous occasions sent us food parcels for months after I had returned to the U.K. The affection I felt for America and for Americans has never diminished.[19]

It may be somewhat surprising to later generations that the predominant relationships formed by the British cadets were with American families. The cadets were often virtually adopted into and became part of local families. Of course relationships between cadets and local girls also developed, but for the most part these relationships occurred within the strict social and moral constraints of the day. Cadets appear to have been happy with social contacts with girls at parties, dances, picnics, and other activities, without an overriding sexual connotation.[20] Some of these relationships developed into permanent unions. Several young women traveled from Texas to England after the war to be married to former cadets, while several cadets returned to Texas and married.

The Terrell War Relief Society took over the care of the British graves in the Oakland Memorial Cemetery. Five women handled the care: Bertha Brewer, Neil Griffith, Mrs. James Marriet, Margaret Bass, and Mary Boyd. Bertha Brewer and her sister Virginia took their father's Model A Ford panel truck to Dallas and brought back two concrete benches for the plot (which greatly overloaded the old truck). The Brewer family owned a flower shop in Terrell and provided flowers for the services. At Palmer's request, Virginia Brewer would ask several local women to attend each service because, as she later related, "military funerals are so bleak."[21]

The school sent a photograph of each service to the families of cadets buried in Terrell. Family members wrote to express their appreciation not only for the photographs, but the obvious care the graves would receive in the future. Mrs. Mollett, mother of the first cadet fatality, wrote:

> It looks extremely nice, and the graves well kept. We cannot express our gratitude to the ladies of the Terrell War Relief Society in mere words, but we find consolation in all they have done and this is what our boy Dick would have wished for most. My husband and daughter join me in heartfelt thanks.[22]

Virtually every family of the cadets buried in the RAF section of the Oakland Memorial Cemetery wrote similar letters. Most of these families knew they would never have an opportunity to visit the graves.

Families also wrote to express appreciation for the generosity shown to sons stationed in Terrell, while former students wrote from exotic places around the world to let those in Terrell know the fate of other students. The wife of Flt. Lt. Harold Taylor wrote to let those in Terrell know her husband had been shot down on his first mission over Europe. A. D. C. Jenkins of Course 4 died in the crash of his Royal Mail flying boat on a flight from Cairo to London. Jenkins' father wrote to friends in Terrell to let them know how much Jenkins had enjoyed his time in Terrell.[23] Len Chapman became an instructor upon his return to England. Chapman and his student were both killed when a German night fighter shot down their trainer. Pilot Officer J. C. Weller wrote from England to let friends in Terrell know that the recent stories of his death were, "a bit exaggerated."[24]

The mother of Andy Wright wrote to let Mr. and Mrs. J. J. Maresh in Terrell know that Wright had been killed on a bombing mission to Stuttgart, Germany. Mrs. Wright wrote, "I thank you very much for the love and kindness you showed Andy, and especially for the lovely photos you sent of him. I have him near me and always will as long as I can see him in the photo you sent. They are so lifelike, better than any we can get done here."[25] Wright was on his last mission before a well-deserved rest. The family learned of Wright's death six months later from the German commandant at Stuttgart. The Germans had given Wright and the other crew members of his bomber a military funeral.

Following graduation, A. B. Eades of Course 9 became an instructor at the Army Airfield in Waco, Texas, and died in a training accident.[26] In February 1944, Terrell residents were relieved to learn that the first commanding officer of No.1 BFTS, Wing Commander Hilton, was a prisoner of war after being shot down over Europe.

The father of Ken Bickers (the cadet lost on his first cross-country flight to Commerce, Texas) wrote to Mr. and Mrs. A. H. Boyd in Terrell to let them know his son had been awarded the Distinguished Flying Cross. Bickers, one of the youngest squadron commanders in the RAF, successfully flew his severely damaged Lancaster bomber back to England after an attack by two German night fighters that killed one of the crew and wounded several others.[27] The top gunner lost both legs in the attack.

Terrell residents were proud to learn that a former student, Flt. Sgt. Arthur Aaron of Course 6, had been awarded the Victoria Cross, Britain's highest military decoration, comparable to the United States Congressional Medal of Honor. Aaron, the pilot of a Stirling bomber, had been grievously wounded in the face and chest on a bombing mission to Turin in northern Italy. Losing blood and in intense pain, Aaron refused shots of morphine and insisted on aiding the crew fly the severely damaged bomber to the nearest Allied base in North Africa. After five hours of struggling to keep the Stirling in the air, Aaron and the second pilot, Allan Larden, managed to belly land the bomber at the Bone airfield in Algeria after several attempts.[28] Ironically, the notice received in Terrell failed to mention that Aaron died of his wounds several hours after landing.[29]

In addition to the awards received by Aaron and Bickers, Flight Officers N. Shott (Course 5), A. A. Vale (Course 2), I. K. Crawford (Course 2), and Pilot Officer F. J. Richardson (Course 5) received the Distinguished Flying Cross (DFC). Sergeant J. A. Christie

(Course 9) received the Distinguished Flying Medal (DFM). At least fifty pilots who trained in Terrell received the Distinguished Flying Cross, Distinguished Flying Medal, or the Air Force Cross.

Ever since the original RAF staff recommended a week's leave between primary and basic training, leaves provided a rare opportunity for cadets to travel and experience various areas of the United States. Restrictions on commercial and military transportation limited travel options, but hitchhiking was still an accepted mode of transportation. Drivers gladly offered rides to servicemen in uniform. Two favorite destinations were San Antonio with its unique Spanish architecture, missions, and the Alamo, and the state capitol in Austin.

Taking leave after primary training, Harry Hewitt and Stan Marshall of Course 25 hitchhiked south to Waco. While wandering around the town, they met the local sheriff, complete with large Stetson hat and cowboy boots. After hearing that Hewitt and Marshall had been constables in England, the sheriff gave the pair a tour of the county jail and offices, complete with several bullet holes in the walls and ceilings. The affable sheriff even lowered his trousers to show the pair an old bullet wound in the buttocks he received while arresting a particularly recalcitrant suspect.

Upon leaving the jail the sheriff hailed a passing station wagon and asked the couple inside to give Hewitt and Marshall a lift further south. The cadets ended up spending several days at the couple's south Texas ranch, swimming and enjoying a new experience: steaks cooked on an outside grill. After traveling on to Austin, the two cadets arrived back in Terrell to resume training.[30]

Some courses received up to ten days of leave and cadets set out on longer trips. Gordon Wenham, Ronnie Ward, Stan Wildman, and Jim Millward of Course 14 hitchhiked to Hollywood in two and one-half days. The young men were briefly arrested in El Paso by Texas Rangers, unfamiliar with RAF uniforms, who thought the cadets were escaped German prisoners of war. In California the cadets met actress Carol Landis on duty at the Hollywood canteen and spoke to actor Peter Lorre, who took an interest in their flying adventures. The group split into pairs for the return trip, which took three and one-half days.[31]

On November 23, 1943, Wing Commander F. B. Tomkins replaced Wing Commander Moxham as the commanding officer of No.1 BFTS. Tomkins had been a member of the Royal Canadian Mounted Police from 1921 through 1923 before joining the RAF in 1925. He served in India until 1929, then entered the reserves until recalled to active duty in 1939.[32]

Two original officers who contributed much to the embryo RAF training facility in Terrell, Squadron Leader Beveridge and Flight Lieutenant Palmer, were reassigned in 1944. Beveridge's wife Robina wrote to the people of Terrell, "From myself, my husband and my family (including my Texan son) thank you for your welcome and all of your kindness to us during our stay in Terrell."[33] Squadron Leader W. Billington replaced Beveridge as the ground supervisor.

Members of the Terrell Episcopal Church of the Good Shepherd gave Palmer a farewell tea and presented him with an engraved sterling silver identification bracelet as a remembrance of his time in Terrell.[34] Flt. Lt. H. C. Sharpe replaced Palmer as the administrative officer.

E. Van Lloyd, the original chief advanced flight instructor, also left the school in 1944. J. E. Castleman, an instructor with considerable seniority with the school, replaced Van Lloyd.

By early 1945 Germany was disintegrating under a continual aerial assault from Army Air Forces bombers by day and RAF bombers by night. Soviet armies entered Germany from the east, while United States, British, and other Allied armies approached from the west and south. Soldiers in Europe whispered the refrain, "Home alive in forty-five."

The expanded flight hours at Terrell included even longer cross-country flights. The final courses embarked on 2,000-mile cross-country trips. Henry Madgwick of Course 24 remembers his long cross-country and a stop in Des Moines, Iowa. His flight consisted of fifteen aircraft and the weather deteriorated after they landed. Fog kept the group in Des Moines for five days. Des Moines turned out to be the main induction center for the Women's Army Corps (WACs) and the RAF cadets had a memorable time waiting for the weather to clear.[35]

In Terrell, training continued under the watchful eye of the greatly expanded RAF Delegation in Washington and the Army Air Forces Flying Training Command.[36] Even though a small base by World War II standards, the Terrell school was not neglected.[37] Even after army cadets no longer trained in Terrell, the army detachment actually increased, since responsibility for the school belonged to the army under lend-lease. By the end of 1944 the army contingent included the commanding officer (a captain), a supply officer, engineering officer, an adjutant (usually a warrant officer), and ten enlisted men. In addition, the school housed the army weather station staff and the medical detachment, which included two surgeons and nine enlisted personnel.

While German armies retreated before the advancing Allies, Japanese forces in the Pacific prepared for a fanatical defense of Iwo Jima and Okinawa. As the school entered its last year of operation, the training schedule continued unabated. On January 15, 1945, two AT-6s collided in midair. Cadets P. E. Allman and R. Griffiths of Course 22 struggled from the spinning wreckage and parachuted safely.

Even during the closing months of the war, the Army Air Forces Flying Training Command continued to conduct periodic inspections of the base. In 1945 the three-day semiannual inspection team from the 32nd Army Flying Training Wing at Perrin Field, Texas, consisted of one lieutenant colonel, one major, one captain, one lieutenant, and two enlisted men.[38] In addition to the semiannual inspections, the army also performed quarterly inspections of the technical and engineering sections. The March 1945 inspection team reported the status of aircraft and equipment at the school to be "excellent."[39]

Army chaplains from various army training facilities in Texas and Oklahoma visited Terrell on a monthly basis to discuss "religious matters." An army civilian employee from the Eighth Service Command visited the base in November 1944 to inspect vehicle tires. In April 1945, a Captain Owens, the sanitary inspector from

Camp Fannin in Tyler, Texas, inspected the base (and made no recommendations).

During an inspection of the army supply unit in March 1945, the inspection team from the Central Flying Training Command at Randolph Field in San Antonio, found serious procedural deficiencies. The Terrell army supply officer (obviously not a career army officer) explained that many of the army procedures did not apply to a civilian school under RAF direction. In addition, the supply officer stated, "The British do not fully understand the ramifications of the AAF supply system and only insist on parts being available when needed; this was being accomplished." The inspection team's reply is not recorded, but can be surmised by the report's final remark, "Full compliance with all AAF regulations is now being effected."[40]

On April 13, 1945, President Franklin Roosevelt died. The next day government offices across the nation closed and the cadets marched into town to join local citizens in a memorial service held at the Episcopal Church of the Good Shepherd.[41] Three weeks later, on May 8, Germany surrendered. The RAF granted open post the next day to commemorate V-E day. The euphoria continued and on the 4th of July, flight operations ceased and the British cadets joined the school staff and Terrell residents in celebrating American Independence Day.

With the conclusion of the war in Europe, the army further reduced its training facilities. In June 1945 the army closed the contract primary flight school located at Garner Field in Uvalde, Texas. Forty-one PT-13s (Stearmans with Lycoming 225-horsepower engines) from the Uvalde school were transferred to Terrell. By this time the original PT-18 primary trainers had been replaced by PT-17s (Stearmans with Continental 220-horsepower engines). During its existence, the Terrell school operated all three Stearman versions utilized by the army: the PT-18, the PT-17, and the PT-13.

Although two of the original BFTS schools had closed by the summer of 1945 (No.2 in Lancaster, California, and No.6 in Ponca City, Oklahoma), the Terrell school remained open.[42] Even after Germany surrendered, it appeared the war in the Pacific would continue well into 1946. The RAF announced the school would remain open until April 1946.[43] But the devastation of two atomic bombs in August 1945 and the resulting Japanese surrender brought the war to a sudden conclusion. All base personnel were granted forty-eight hours' leave to commemorate the end of the war.[44]

Orders were received to close No.1 BFTS on September 11, 1945. Wing Commander T. O. Prickett, a former bomber pilot in the Middle East and Malta, had assumed command of the unit on August 7, 1945, but in reality only supervised the closing of the school. A large crowd watched as Course 25 marched to the last wings parade on August 24. Air Marshal Douglas Colyer of the RAF Delegation in Washington reviewed the wing and delivered the final address under a hot deep-blue Texas sky dotted with white puffy cumulus clouds. As the warm breeze ruffled the RAF flag flying from the mobile flagpole, Colyer expressed "The fervent hope that friendship between the United States and England as it now exists would forever abide, making for the peace and prosperity of the world."[45] Courses 26 and 27 continued training, but left when the school closed. Cadets in these two courses were given the option to complete training in England or return to civilian life. The RAF canceled Course 28, scheduled to arrive in Terrell in late August.

A final, albeit premature, memorial service took place on September 3, 1945, at the Oakland Memorial Cemetery for the eighteen RAF cadets buried there. That afternoon an AT-6 failed to return from a cross-country flight to San Marcos, Texas. Searchers found the wreckage of the Harvard in Lake Travis near Austin the next day. Thomas Beedie and Raymond Botcher joined their comrades in the Oakland Memorial Cemetery. The first cadet fatality had occurred before the United States entered the war, and the last two fatalities occurred after the war ended.

The piano, radio, records, and other items originally donated for the recreation hall were given to the Red Cross for use in the Ashburn General Hospital in McKinney, Texas. The RAF staff took the mobile flagpole used in so many graduation ceremonies and mounted it behind the RAF memorial at the Oakland Memorial Cemetery.[46]

Wing Commander Prickett wrote open letters to the citizens of both Terrell and Dallas expressing thanks for the many signs of friendship and hospitality shown the British cadets during the school's four-year existence. He said, "There are so many kindnesses we remember, our sojourn here has provided for so many pleasant memories that it is difficult for us to adequately express our feelings as we say goodbye."[47]

The editor of the *Terrell Daily Tribune* replied, "To the RAF let us say your friendly courteous manner and your cooperation and interest in our civic and social life has made you many friends who regret having you leave our midst."[48] The *Dallas Morning News* editorialized, "The little school whose runways cross-stitched the Kaufman County grasses and blackland was more than an emergency training base. It turned out to be a profitable bond between two great nations."[49]

The school closed and the RAF staff and remaining cadets left Terrell on the afternoon of September 10, 1945, on several additional cars added to the Sunshine Special. A small army contingent remained behind to inventory and supervise the disposition of the government property. At the end of the month the last of the army personnel locked the buildings and departed.

The buildings are gone now. Even the cotton fields are mostly gone, replaced by grass pastures or other diverse crops. The Terrell airport is surrounded by modern highways with high-speed traffic and sprawling industrial plants. The only reminder of the RAF presence is the Oakland Memorial Cemetery plot with its twenty headstones and a small stone memorial dedicated by Lord Halifax in April 1942. On the simple monument is an inscription taken from Rupert Brooke's poem, *The Soldier:* "Some corner of a foreign field that is forever England."

---

1. *Terrell Daily Tribune,* June 6, 1944.

2. "History of the 2564th Army Air Forces Base Unit, 1 Nov 44 - 31 Dec 44," located in Maxwell, microfilm roll A2281, 12.

3. ORB, February 20, 1943, February 22, 1943.

4. Eric Gill, conversation with the author, September 11, 2000.

5. Ben Brown, "Terrell Tales No.23," published in the No.1 BFTS Association newsletter.

6. Arthur Ridge, interview by the author, Dallas, Texas, January 29, 2000. The field Ridge landed in became famous thirty years later as Southfork Ranch, the setting for the television series *Dallas.*

7. Ray Flennekin, interview by the author.

8. Frank Jones, "Terrell Tales No.30," published in the No.1 BFTS Association newsletter.

9. *Dallas Morning News,* June 1, 1944.

10. Ben Brown, phone interview by the author, February 12, 2000.

11. Related by Virginia Brewer, a friend of Langston, in an interview by the author, Canton, Texas, September 10, 2000.

12. Don Ashby, "Terrell Tales No. 37," published in the No.1 BFTS Association newsletter.

13. Ted Nieass, "Terrell Tales No. 29," published in the No.1 BFTS Association newsletter.

14. Nelson Grisham, as well as several other Terrell instructors, joined the new Air Transport Command later in the war and went on to fly transports around the world.

15. *Terrell Daily Tribune,* August 26, 1944.

16. *Dallas Morning News,* September 9, 1945.

17. Guinn, compilation of student recollections.

18. *Terrell Daily Tribune,* May 30, 1945.

19. Guinn, compilation of student recollections.

20. Although several unplanned pregnancies did occur. Henry Madgwick, interview by the author, Terrell, Texas, August 10, 1993.

21. Virginia Brewer, unpublished paper titled, "RAF Cemetery, Terrell, Texas," June 1991, in the possession of the author.

22. *Terrell Daily Tribune,* December 19, 1942.

23. Ibid., October 31, 1942

24. Ibid., July 29, 1943.

25. Ibid., November 25, 1944.

26. While as many as 450 British cadets from the Arnold Scheme were retained as instructors, primarily in the Southeast Training Command, relatively few BFTS graduates taught at army schools. The few graduates of No.1 BFTS retained as instructors usually taught at the Waco Army Airfield, Majors Field in Greenville, or Randolph Field in San Antonio.

27. Bickers lied about his age in order to join the British Army, then trans-

ferred to the RAF when he was nineteen.

28. The attack, initially attributed to a German night fighter, actually came from the rear gunner of another Stirling bomber. Chaz Bowyer, "Bomber VC, the Story of Flt Sgt A.L. Aaron, VC, DFM," *Aircraft Illustrated Extra, Bombers of World War II*, no. 10; 34-39.

29. *Terrell Daily Tribune*, November 11, 1943.

30. Harry Hewitt, "Terrell Tales" published in the No.1 BFTS Association newsletter.

31. Jim Millward, "Terrell Tales" published in the No.1 BFTS Association newsletter.

32. A resume for Tomkins is located in Maxwell, "History of the 321st AAFFDT," Report dated 1 Nov 44 - 31 Dec 44, 12. Tomkins had 5,946 hours of flight time when he arrived in Terrell.

33. *Terrell Daily Tribune*, September 20, 1944.

34. Ibid., April 16, 1944.

35. Henry Madgwick, interview by author, August 10, 1993.

36. In July 1942 the headquarters of the Army Air Forces Flying Training Command relocated from Washington, D.C., to the Texas and Pacific building in Fort Worth, Texas, where it remained during World War II. *Fort Worth Star Telegram*, February 20, 1944.

37. By comparison, the United States Navy constructed a new primary pilot training base in Peru, Indiana, which had a complement of 300 Stearmans in 1944 and was only one of several navy primary training bases. James, *Teacher Wore a Parachute*, 127-29.

38. "History of the 2564th AAFBU, 1 July 45 - 30 Sep 45" Maxwell, microfilm roll A2281.

39. ORB, March 5, 1945.

40. "History of the 2564th AAFBU, 1 Mar 45 - 30 Apr 45" Maxwell, microfilm roll A2281.

41. Ibid. Also ORB, April 13, 14, 1945, and *Terrell Daily Tribune*, April 14, 1945.

42. The Arnold Scheme ended in March 1943 and the Towers Scheme continued until September 1945.

43. *Terrell Daily Tribune*, August 2, 1945.

44. Ibid., August 16, 1945; ORB, August 15, 1945.

45. Ibid., August 24, 1945.

46. *Dallas Morning News*, September 11, 1945.

47. *Terrell Daily Tribune*, September 7, 1945.

48. Ibid., September 10, 1945.

49. *Dallas Morning News*, August 23, 1945.

CHAPTER 8

EPILOGUE

One of the ironies of wartime RAF pilot training is that graduates of early courses from No.1 BFTS suffered heavy losses after posting to operational squadrons due to the intensity of the fighting, while many graduates of later courses saw little or no action. Bert Allam used both official and unofficial sources after the war to trace the original thirty-three ex-British Army transfers who joined Course 4 in Terrell. Only seven survived the war.[1] Another Terrell graduate, Douglas Sivyer, traced the operational records of the graduates of Course 3. Of the thirty-eight graduates, only fourteen survived the war. The list includes details of the last flights of those lost. Many of the descriptions contain nothing more than the poignant epitaph, "failed to return."[2]

Eight graduates of Course 3 attended an Operational Training Unit (OTU) on Spitfires. One of the pilots, Eddie McCann, flew with 131 and 165 Squadrons at Tangmere and then 232 Squadron in the Mediterranean where he escorted American medium bombers. Of the others trained on Spitfires, Johnny Gallon and Frank Seeley were killed while operating in 11 Group (England); Vernon Brooker, Blondie Reeves, and George Richardson were killed in North Africa; Bob Wood was killed in Malta, and Peter King in Sicily. Of the original eight, only McCann survived the war.[3]

Ken Bickers, the cadet lost on his first cross-country flight to Commerce, Texas, and later awarded the Distinguished Flying Cross, disappeared on a bombing mission to Berlin in March 1944. The final resting place of Bickers and his entire crew is unknown. On the same night Bickers disappeared, his old friend from Course 4, Flt. Lt. L. C. J. "Bonzo"

144

Brodrick and seventy-five other POWs tunneled out of the Stalag Luft 3 prison camp in what has become known as "The Great Escape." Brodrick avoided the fate of fifty of the escapees who were recaptured and executed by the Gestapo.[4] Jack Bolter of Course 4 and his entire bomber crew disappeared over Germany in March 1945, less than two months before the end of the war in Europe.

On his return to England following graduation, Bert Allam became an instructor, much to his dismay. In retrospect this assignment may have saved him from the fate of so many other members of Course 4. Later in the war Allam joined a Lancaster bomber squadron and flew missions over Germany.

Toward the end of the war, with the Axis on the defensive, the Allies enjoyed aerial supremacy over virtually every front. With an ample supply of pilots, graduates of flight schools were often delayed in holding centers waiting for operational postings. Some found no openings at all. Henry Madgwick graduated with Course 24 in 1945 and never saw operational service.[5] Several graduates from Courses 16 through 20 were retrained in England to fly gliders and participated in Operation Varsity, the crossing of the Rhine. At least three Terrell graduates, W. H. Paul, P. N. Hyde, and W. F. Murphy, were killed in this operation.[6]

After the war former cadets of No.1 BFTS and staff personnel dispersed around the world. Flight Lieutenant Palmer served in Cairo, Egypt, in the Judge Advocate General's office.[7] He later became the head of the RAF legal department and retired as an air commodore (the equivalent of a brigadier general). Sir John Gingell of Course 23 and later president of No.1 BFTS Association in England, attained the rank of air chief marshal (the same rank as a four-star general) and became Black Rod in the House of Lords. Michael Giddings of Course 1 earned both the DFC and AFC and became an air marshal (the same rank as a lieutenant general). Frank Miller, the former art student and designer of the school crest, became a successful architect in Australia. Ray England, the top cadet of Course 9 and later an instructor at the Waco Army Airfield, became the chairman and chief executive of Jaguar Motors in 1972. Thomas Round of Course 10 also served as an instructor assigned to the U.S. Army Air Forces and after the war became an internationally acclaimed operatic tenor. British actor Robert Hardy, noted for his portrayals of Winston Churchill and starring role in the Public Broadcasting System television series *All Creatures Great and Small* trained with Course 27, one of the last two courses that did not graduate at Terrell.

Alan Bramson, the top cadet of Course 16 and the cadet who invented the story of being bounced by the army P-51 to cover the fact he had slammed his navigator and good friend into the canopy of their Harvard, became an instructor upon his return to England. After the war Bramson continued in the aviation field. He has written more than twenty-two aviation books and articles, including a well-received series of flight training manuals. At the age of seventy-eight Bramson continued to consult regularly on commercial aviation matters, and was still certified to fly the most modern four-engine jet transports.

Besides Palmer, Giddings, and Sir John Gingell who rose to prominent rank in the RAF, other Terrell graduates stayed in the RAF and flew operationally after the war. Arthur Ridge of Course 25 flew in the Berlin Airlift. Jim Forteith of Course 9 flew missions in Burma and later in Malaysia against communist insurgents. Eric Gill of Course 20 flew weather reconnaissance missions in the new Avro Lincoln. Several RAF pilots who had trained in Terrell joined the Volunteer Reserve after the war and were recalled to duty during the Korean War. One of these, William Ellis of Course 12, flew the new Gloster Meteor jet with No.504 City of Nottingham Royal Auxiliary Air Force Squadron and served two years on active duty during the Korean War.

Most former Terrell students returned to a diverse range of civilian occupations after the war, while some continued to fly professionally. Ralph Breyfogle, an American cadet with Course 18, joined United Airlines as a copilot in 1946 and flew for the next thirty-four years, before retiring as a senior captain with more than 20,000 hours of flight time. Charles Gray of Course 10 joined BOAC and retired as a senior captain. Not satisfied with retirement, Gray then joined Gulf Air as senior training captain.

After the war several former cadets returned to the United States to live. Eric Gill returned to Dallas, married, and received a degree in petroleum engineering from Southern Methodist University. Jim Forteith returned to Dallas and married a lady he originally met at a dance sponsored by the Hockaday School during the war. Henry Madgwick returned to Terrell, married, and entered the insurance business. Citizens elected Madgwick mayor of Terrell in 1998 and again in 2000 (when he ran unopposed). Arthur Ridge retired from the RAF then moved to Murphy, Texas, north of Dallas. Ridge now lives less than two miles from the field in which he landed on his first solo cross-country flight and encountered the large black woman with the red bandana.[8]

Several of the instructors who left the school during the war joined the fledgling Air Transport Command and flew missions around the world including the treacherous Hump over the Himalayas between India and China. After the war the former civilian instructors reflected the nation's return to a peacetime economy. As with most of the nation's returning servicemen, the majority of the former instructors went to work for various private companies. Bill Brookover went into the oil business in West Texas and New Mexico, while Ray Flenniken retired after twenty-one years with General Motors.

Some of the former instructors continued to fly. Garnett Howell, a former advanced instructor at the school, joined the newly formed United Nations and flew in Mexico and Europe. The UN then sent Howell to instruct in Africa where several of his students went on to become senior captains with African national airlines.[9] Another instructor, M. S. Norwood, managed the Terrell airport in the 1960s.

Finding any flying job for a woman pilot in the 1940s proved to be virtually impossible, so Louise Sacchi became a navigation instructor at No. 1 BFTS. After the war, Sacchi returned home to Pennsylvania and became a flight instructor. In 1962 she began a sixteen-year career ferrying new private aircraft overseas. By the time she retired in 1978 Sacchi had ferried 333 aircraft, mostly Beachcrafts, over both the Atlantic and Pacific oceans, held several speed records, and had written two books. She passed away in 1999 at the age of 83.[10]

Some of the postwar careers took unexpected turns. After the war Lloyd Nolen, a former advanced instructor, continued to fly as a crop duster in the Rio Grande valley of Texas.[11] In 1951 Nolen and four friends purchased a surplus P-51 Mustang fighter for $2,500 to fly for fun. Several years later the group acquired two surplus Grumman F8F Bearcats. Developed late in the war, the Bearcat was one of the last piston engine fighters. The group, jokingly called the Confederate Air Force, was shocked to discover that the government had systematically destroyed most of the tens of thousands of military aircraft built during the war. The Confederate Air Force set out to find, restore, and preserve in flying condition as many types of World War II aircraft as possible.

At the beginning of the twenty-first century the Confederate Air Force, with headquarters in Midland, Texas, was the largest flying museum in the world, and in 2002 became the Commemorative Air Force. The Commemorative Air Force collection contains military aircraft from Allied as well as Axis nations, and includes the only flying Boeing B-29 Superfortress in the world. The B-29 was the largest and most sophisticated bomber that was built during World War II.

The British government recognized Major Long, Luckey, and Van Lloyd for their wartime services. Long and Luckey became honorary members of the Civil Division of The Most Excellent Order of the British Empire (OBE), while Van Lloyd became a Member of the Order of the British Empire (MBE). Long also received the President's Certificate of Merit from the United States. Harding Lawrence, former head of the Link trainer department and later assistant director of the school, became the president and CEO of Braniff Airways.

Long sold his interest in the Dallas Aviation School after the war, but continued in the aviation field. Long and Gen. Robert J.

Smith had formed a new feeder airline, Essair, which became Pioneer Airlines in 1946. Pioneer operated in Texas and New Mexico until it merged with Continental Airlines in 1955.[12] At the time of his death in Dallas on August 19, 1976, Long served on the board of directors of Gates Learjet Corporation.[13] His career had literally spanned the breadth of aviation history from the ninety horsepower, fabric-covered JN-4D Jenny of World War I to the age of the corporate business jet.

As the men and women of No. 1 BFTS returned to civilian life, the military quickly dismantled the former flying training command. After the war, the training aircraft found new roles in a limited civilian market, unlike the massive bombers and powerful fighters, which were reduced to scrap by the thousands.

Stearmans initially found a home in numerous local flight schools spawned by the new GI Bill. William Pulley, owner of the first postwar flight school in Arlington, Texas, operated a fleet of surplus Stearmans. Asked about the purchase price, Pulley remarked almost apologetically, "Well you see mine were some of the last off the assembly line, low time and hardly used by the military, so I had to pay top dollar; paid $200 each for mine."[14] Only months before, during the war, Stearmans had cost the United States government around $10,000 each. Even with the low initial cost, the big open cockpit Stearmans were just not as efficient for civilian pilot training as the newer postwar Pipers, Cessnas, Taylorcrafts, and Aeroncas and did not last long in their traditional role as trainers.

The Stearman's real niche came as crop dusters in the postwar agricultural boom. Operators removed the front cockpit, installed a hopper tank, associated spray booms, and almost always a larger engine of 300 or even 450 horsepower. The low level work proved hazardous to both pilots and aircraft, and the corrosive chemicals quickly ate away at the Stearmans' steel tube frames. Because of the low initial cost, most operators bought several Stearmans and then cannibalized them in order to keep others flying, until those too, simply wore out.

By the 1960s when specialized agricultural aircraft began to be produced, the carcasses of derelict Stearmans were permanent fixtures at small airports across the southern and southwestern United States, the wind perpetually sighing through the corroded frames and rotted wood, accompanied by the gentle flapping of the tattered remains of the once tight cotton fabric covering. Then came a renewed interest in the war and things aeronautical and martial, and almost overnight a virtual swarm of museum representatives, collectors, restorers, and new warbird enthusiasts descended on the abandoned carcasses and spirited them away to restoration centers around the country.

After years of work, not to mention considerable expenditure, Stearmans began to reappear in like-new condition as prized possessions. Many of these restored Stearmans now sport larger engines, elaborate instruments, and to the purist's dismay, electrical systems, starters, and even radios. Most, however, tend to be faithful to the original product, even to the military paint schemes and various stenciled placards and labels.

Unfortunately the Vultee Valiant's tarnished (and many would argue undeserved) reputation followed it after the war. Because of this reputation and the higher operating costs due to its larger engine, the Vultee never found a niche with postwar flyers and most were simply scrapped. But the late blooming interest in restoring warbirds also embraced the remaining, almost forgotten, Vultees and those that had escaped the scrap heap were lovingly and lavishly restored. Several BT-13s were superficially modified to resemble Japanese "Val" dive bombers and appeared in movies such as *Tora, Tora, Tora.* Although now found in much fewer numbers than the once contemporary Stearmans, Vultees are almost always restored to their original military configuration.

Unlike the other trainers, the AT-6 enjoyed both a civilian and a continued military career after the war. Although many were sold as surplus on the civilian market, the AT-6 was designated by the United States as the principal postwar military trainer. In addition, AT-6s were provided under various military assistance programs to

friendly foreign governments. Such was the demand for the trainers that the United States was forced to buy back some AT-6s from
the civilian market (at greatly inflated prices).[15]

In Canada, Canadian Car and Foundry reintroduced production of the Harvard, which continued from 1952 until 1954. North
American completely rebuilt and upgraded older AT-6s, which were
then redesignated T-6Gs (the "A" designation having been
dropped). The T-6 served in Korea as an observation aircraft and
then continued with the United States military until the late 1950s,
and with some foreign military services into the 1970s.[16] Civilian
AT-6s raced in a separate class at the revived National Air Races in
the late 1940s and later at the Reno Air Races. Today numerous
immaculately restored AT-6s are found in flight museums, aircraft
collections, and in the hands of private owners.

After the war, a group of Terrell businessmen purchased the
Kaufman County airport in an action reminiscent of the original
land purchase and turned the airport over to the city.[17] The dirt
and gravel roads were steadily improved over the years; now multi-
lane highways provide access to the airport. The original frame
buildings disappeared in a sea of industrial expansion and a four-
lane road now cuts through the original school site to provide access to industrial plants. The last building at the school, the
operations building, survived as the airport management office into
the late 1960s, then was torn down. The third hangar was converted
to commercial use, then later burned to the ground. The two original hangars were incorporated into manufacturing facilities. The
distinctive curved roofs were still discernable in 2002, but few noticed. Curious metal rods imbedded in the wide concrete apron
now used to store material and park heavy trailers can still be seen.
These tie downs once secured scores of trainers that taught young
British students to fly.

After the war the school returned the leased auxiliary fields to
the landowners. The building at Griffin Field served as a barn for
several decades until it collapsed from neglect. The Bass Drug store
is still in Terrell, but the beautiful wood counter and soda fountain

are gone. With the postwar growth in air travel and the new interstate highway system, the Texas and Pacific railroad discontinued passenger service to Terrell. Years later the city tore down the old passenger terminal, originally constructed in 1901 and so familiar to the British cadets. This action still angers many Terrell residents.

The BFTS program in the United States constituted a relatively small portion of wartime pilot training. Between September 1939 and September 1945, 62,909 pilots were trained for the RAF, plus an additional 54,760 pilots for various Commonwealth air forces, for a total of 117,669.[18] The majority of these pilots trained in overseas training facilities. The largest contingent, 54,269 pilots, trained in Canada (22,608 RAF and 32,201 from Commonwealth countries). A total of 13,673 RAF pilots trained in the United States in the three programs, the Arnold Scheme, the Towers Scheme, and the BFTS schools.[19] The six BFTS schools graduated 6,602 pilots for the RAF, and 551 AAF pilots.[20] Records for individual schools, however, are often incomplete.

For a World War II training organization that contained civilian, United States Army Air Forces, and Royal Air Force components, official records for No.1 BFTS are sketchy. The RAF's Operations Record Book (ORB) in the archives of the Public Record Office in London is fairly complete for middle courses, but the original writer (probably Palmer) frankly admits that the initial entries were written twenty-one months after the opening of the school from the memory of those who were there. He states, "[the record] must of necessity present in outline only the history of the unit."[21] The reason given is that the small size of the original staff did not allow time for detailed record keeping. From Course 16 on, the records are also incomplete. A spokesman for the Public Record Office told Dr. Gilbert S. Guinn, professor emeritus in history at Lander University in Greenwood, South Carolina, that an overzealous employee attempted to clean out the records years ago and, "apparently overdid it."

The official United States Air Force archives at Maxwell Air Force Base in Alabama contains only a review of the school before the

American cadets arrived with Course 13. The army records are fairly complete after this time, but concentrate on details of the army unit and contain some obvious errors. In one place the army records refer to eleven courses at Terrell that included AAF cadets, while two other references refer to eight courses with AAF cadets. The actual number is seven courses.

The records for the Terrell Aviation School no longer exist. After the school closed, the records were presumably moved to the Dallas Aviation School offices at Love Field in Dallas. Henry Madgwick, a former cadet and mayor of Terrell from 1998 to 2002, believes the records were destroyed in a fire. Others do not accept this theory. An American Airlines DC-6, however, crashed at Love Field in November 1949 on a flight from New York to Mexico City. The resulting fires at the northeast corner of Love Field destroyed several buildings including one belonging to the Dallas Aviation School.[22]

There is also no official accounting of the number of students who trained at No.1 BFTS or the actual number of graduates. Some of the best sources of information are the photographs of each class kept by the Bass Drug store in Terrell (Bass developed the photos) and now in the Terrell Public Library. These photos taken at the beginning of each course show a total of 2,140 cadets from Course 1 through Course 27. This number includes 128 Army Air Forces cadets. Twenty additional cadets, ten RAF and ten AAF, joined No.1 BFTS when No.6 BFTS in Ponca City, Oklahoma, closed in April 1944. This results in a total of 2,160 cadets, assuming everyone was present for the photographs. Additional adjustments, however, are still necessary.

Cadets from the short-lived No.7 BFTS in Sweetwater, Texas (where there was only one primary course), were sent to other schools to continue training. Apparently twelve to fifteen cadets from Sweetwater joined Course 10 in Terrell at the end of primary training (the records are again unclear).[23] Several RAF students also joined No.1 BFTS after elimination from army schools in the Arnold Scheme. The best estimate of the total number of cadets trained at No.1 BFTS, therefore, is between 2,180 and 2,200.

The actual number of graduates is also difficult to determine. Early courses experienced wash-out rates that varied from fifteen percent to fifty-one percent. Some later courses experienced extremely low wash-out rates. An August 25, 1945, *Dallas Morning News* article on the closing of the school indicates that a total of 1,470 pilots graduated during the school's four-year operation. Presumably this number came from the school records, but the article gives no source for the information. Using an average of twenty-five percent failures for RAF cadets and fifteen percent for AAF cadets and subtracting Courses 26 and 27, which did not graduate due to the ending of the war, gives an estimate of 1,480 graduates, which is very close to the number cited in the *Dallas Morning News* article.

Former cadets of No.1 BFTS met in London in 1950 and again in 1962. In 1984 Bert Allam and Alan Bramson formed the No.1 BFTS Association in England. The association sponsors regular meetings, publishes a newsletter, and organizes reunions of former No.1 BFTS cadets.

In Texas, Eric Gill, Nickey Maumovich, Bill Brookover, and several others, formed the North American chapter of the No.1 BFTS Association. The two organizations held joint reunions in 1985, 1987, 1991, and 1995, which alternated between England and Texas. At each reunion a list of distinguished graduates is read along with the names of the commanding officers (the name of the last commanding officer, Wing Commander Prickett, always receives a round of good natured "boos" as the officer who presided over closing No.1 BFTS).

After the war Bertha Brewer and her sister Virginia cared for the British graves in the Oakland Memorial Cemetery until Bertha's death in 1976. Virginia then continued the practice and placed fresh flowers on each grave at Christmas and special occasions until the early 1990s. Others continue to place flowers on the graves and a memorial service is still held each October at the cemetery. The religious symbols on the individual headstones tell their own stories. There are eighteen Christian crosses, one Jewish Star of

David, and one headstone without a symbol, belonging to an agnostic.

The North American No.1 BFTS Association set up a large display in the Terrell Heritage Society museum located in the old Carnegie library in Terrell. Exhibits include class photographs, uniforms, maps, and a model of the airfield as it appeared during the war. A bench in front of the Terrell Library and a plaque presented to the city by the British and North American No.1 BFTS associations commemorates the strong ties between the former British cadets and the city of Terrell.

More than fifty-five years after the closing of the school, the story of No.1 BFTS continued to live on. In 1997 Beth Lawless, an elementary school teacher in Rattan, Oklahoma, asked her sixth grade reading class to select a topic for a research project. One student had heard his grandfather tell the story of an airplane crash in the nearby mountains during World War II. The aircraft might have been an army bomber. The class decided to research the story and quickly learned that the crash involved the two AT-6s from No.1 BFTS in Terrell that crashed on February 20, 1943.

The scope of the project grew and finally involved two sixth-grade reading classes. Twelve students in the 1997-98 class and eleven students in the 1998-99 class participated in the project. At the students' request, the Smithsonian Institute in Washington provided information on the aircraft. The class contacted the British Embassy in Washington, the Public Record Office in London, and the Air Force archives at Maxwell Air Force Base in Alabama. Henry Madgwick in Terrell and others in the North American No.1 BFTS Association provided additional information. At the conclusion of the project, the classes produced a well-written final report, then decided to raise money to erect a memorial to the four British cadets who died in the Kiamichi mountains. The project now became a community project.

The classes asked the British Broadcasting Corporation in London to help locate any surviving relatives of the crash victims. The story aired by the BBC generated considerable interest. Men and women throughout Great Britain were deeply moved to learn that elementary school children in a small Oklahoma town no one had ever heard of cared enough to erect a memorial to young British flyers who had died more than fifty years earlier. Following the publicity, British Airways offered to fly the relatives to Dallas for the dedication ceremony.

On February 20, 2000, exactly fifty-seven years after the crashes, a large crowd estimated at more than 700, gathered just outside Moyers, Oklahoma, to dedicate the grey granite memorial, under clear blue skies. The beautiful day and warm temperature offered a stark contrast to the cold misty overcast day on February 20, 1943. At the ceremony, the Antlers, Oklahoma, high school band played, "God Save the Queen" and the "Star Spangled Banner," while a National Guard honor guard from the Choctaw Nation presented the colors. Buglers played both the British "Last Post" and the American "Taps." The Lord Mayor of the London Borough of Redbridge, complete in the official robes of office, and the New Zealand Military Attache from Washington, D.C. attended. Seventeen relatives of the four cadets sat in several rows of metal chairs arranged under a canvas awning. Behind the relatives sat John Wall from New Zealand and Gordon Wright from England, the cadets in the other AT-6 that made a precautionary landing in a nearby valley.[24]

The story of No.1 BFTS involves more than the story of young men learning to fly. At the international level, it is the story of "One of the greatest wartime cooperative ventures ever undertaken between nations."[25] Aircrew training, along with other cooperative ventures such as lend-lease, cemented the alliance between Great Britain and the United States that transcended national interest and continued after the war, throughout the cold war, and exists to this day. At the local level, Terrell citizens and the British cadets formed a unique and long lasting bond.

Flight Lieutenant Palmer later commented on the lasting benefits of the BFTS program, "They have contributed much to Anglo-American understanding, interest and good will. And they have drawn closer the bonds of friendship, a friendship which will grow and endure long after the experiences on which it was founded have been forgotten."[26]

Looking back after almost sixty years, Bert Allam of Course 4 remarked, "What did Terrell give me? Six wonderful months in pleasant surroundings, doing what I had wanted to do (learn to fly) in company with some of the most enjoyable companions I have ever had, and making lasting friendships with some of the most likeable and hospitable people in the world."[27] These comments have been echoed by scores of former students. Ben Brown, an American cadet in Course 18, said simply, "The time at Terrell was the best six months of my life."[28]

Although the No.1 BFTS associations on both sides of the Atlantic continue to be active into the twenty-first century, in October 2000 (the same year Dallas refurbished and reinstalled the neon outlined flying red horse sign on top of the old Magnolia Petroleum building) the No.1 BFTS Association in England and the North American Association hosted what many believe will be the last joint reunion of No.1 BFTS.

Appropriately, the remaining former students and school personnel met in Terrell, Texas, for the last time.

---

1. Ex-British Army personnel in the RAF had unique six-digit serial numbers, which stood out prominently on various official lists including casualty lists.

2. Included with an unpublished manuscript by Henry Madgwick, Terrell, Texas, in the possession of the author.

3. Guinn, "BFTS No.1 The Influence of Events."

4. Allam, "Into the Wild Blue Yonder."

5. Henry Madgwick, interview by the author, Terrell, Texas, August 10, 1993.

6. Records in the possession of Eric Gill, a former cadet in Course 20, now living in Dallas.

7. *Terrell Daily Tribune*, September 15, 1945.

8. Arthur Ridge, interview by the author, Dallas, Texas, January 29, 2000.

9. Jane Howell, phone interview by the author, December 18, 2000.

10. No.1 BFTS Association newsletter, June 2000.

11. Because he wore glasses, Nolen could not fly in the armed forces during the war, or for the airlines after the war. Lloyd Nolen passed away in 1991.

12. Marvin Krieger, the former Hollywood animator and No.1 BFTS navigation instructor, designed the logo for Pioneer Airlines. George W. Cearley, *A Pictorial History of Airline Service at Dallas Love Field* (Dallas: np, 1989), 61.

13. *Dallas Morning News*, August 21, 1976.

14. William (Bill) Pulley conversation with the author, Arlington, Texas, August 1967.

15. Leo Kohn, *The Story of the Texan* (Appleton, WI: Aviation Pubs, 1989), xiii.

16. Ibid.

17. *Terrell Daily Tribune*, October 6, 1945, October 16, 1945, November 6, 1945, and January 15, 1946.

18. British Air Ministry, *Flying Training 1939-1945, Vol.I - Policy and Planning.* A.H.B. Air Publication 3233, 279. In comparison, the United States Army trained 193,440 pilots between 1939 and 1945 according to the Smithsonian National Air and Space Museum. Of this number 44,958 Army pilots were trained in Texas between January 1, 1942, and May 1, 1944. *Texas Almanac 1945-1946* (Dallas: A. H. Belo Corporation, 1945), 78.

19. British Air Ministry, "Flying Training, 1939-1945" A.H.B. Air Publication 3233. This number includes 598 Americans who underwent refresher training to qualify for entry into the RAF before the United States entered the war.

20. "Report on Twenty-Fifth Aug/45 Output British Flying Training Schools in the U.S.A." located in AIR 20/1387, Public Record Office, London.

21. ORB, Introduction, 2.

22. *Dallas Morning News*, August 13, 1950.

23. The final report for Course 10 refers to an intake of sixty-five, while the original course report shows an intake of fifty-three. Since the time is correct and other references mention Sweetwater students joining Course 10 in Terrell, the difference between the original report and the final report is probably due to the Sweetwater students. But it is unclear if the original fifty-three were new students or fifty new students and three holdovers, thus the estimate of twelve to fifteen students from Sweetwater.

24. "AT-6s Crash Near Moyers During WW II." Sixth grade reading project Rattan, Oklahoma elementary school 1997-98, copy located in the Terrell Public Library.

25. Guinn, "British Aircrew Training," 17.

26. Flt. Lt. M. W. Palmer, "British Flying Training Schools in America," *Transatlantic*, (April 1945), 27.

27. Bert Allam, letter to the author, January 12, 2000.

28. Ben Brown, phone interview by the author, February 12, 2000.

APPENDIX A

LIST OF FATALITIES

Twenty-four men died while training at No.1 BFTS between 1941 and 1945. Nineteen British RAF cadets, three civilian instructors, and one Army Air Forces cadet died in flying accidents. One British cadet died of natural causes. The bodies of the three instructors and one army cadet were returned to their homes in various parts of the United States for burial. The twenty British cadets are buried in the Oakland Memorial Cemetery in Terrell.

November 10, 1941
Richard D. Mollett

AND SO HE PASSED OVER
A VALIANT YOUNG HEART
HIS SPIRIT LIVES ON

The crash occurred at night just after takeoff four miles south of the airport. Mollett was only two days from graduation. He apparently became disoriented after takeoff.

January 18, 1942
William L. Ibbs

AGE 21
A LOVING SON, GOOD AND KIND
A BEAUTIFUL MEMORY LEFT BEHIND

The crash occurred five miles from Cumby, Texas, during a night cross-country flight. Ibbs became lost and contacted the Terrell tower and received directions to the field, but he ran out of fuel and crashed before reaching Terrell. Ibbs died only two days from graduation.

January 21, 1942
George I. Hanson

HE HAD A NATURE YOU
COULDN'T HELP LOVING
AND A HEART THAT
WAS PURER THAN GOLD

T.O. Somerville, Instructor
The PT-18 crashed three miles north of Kaufman after an engine failure at low altitude.

February 7, 1942
Ramond A. Berry

THY WILL BE DONE

Leonard G. Blower

DEAR FRIEND OF MINE
I'LL WALK BESIDE YOU
TO THE HOLY CITY
MUM, DAD AND FAMILY

Two AT-6s collided in midair at 2:30 in the afternoon six miles north of Wills Point.

February 14, 1942
Aubrey R. Atkins

ONE OF THE DEAREST,
ONE OF THE BEST,
NOW IN GOD'S KEEPING
SAFE AT REST

The aircraft crashed two miles west of the field at 4:15 in the morning during routine night flying.

May 28, 1942
James Craig

PEACEFULLY SLEEPING
FAR AWAY FROM HOME
AND HIS DEAR ONES

Three aircraft were buzzing the Wills Point auxiliary field at 9:00 in the morning when Craig's aircraft struck the beacon light.

September 17, 1942
Geoffrey M. Harris

IN UNFADING MEMORY OF
OUR DARLING GEOFFREY
PEACE TO HIS SWEET SOUL

The aircraft emerged from heavy clouds about 7:00 in the evening in a steep dive. Harris bailed out but apparently struck the tail of the aircraft. A local doctor saw the parachute descending and stopped to render aid, but Harris was already dead when he landed.

October 27, 1942
Allan S. Gadd

GOODBYE BELOVED, SLEEP
ON AND TAKE THY REST.
UNTIL WE MEET AGAIN.
CONSTANCE

Thomas Travers

HE GAVE HIS LIFE IN
THE CAUSE OF FREEDOM

Two aircraft collided while shifting position during formation flying west of Wills Point at 3:00 in the afternoon.

February 1, 1943
Alan R. Langston

HE WILLINGLY SERVED
HIS COUNTRY IN THE
CAUSE OF FREEDOM

During night flying practice the aircraft taxied into a stock tank on the Terrell airfield and overturned. Langston drowned before help could arrive.

February 20, 1943
Vincent H. Cockman

FEARLESS AND GAY,
INTO GOD'S ARMS HE FLEW
HE DIED IN THE
SUPREME ENDEAVOUR

Frank R.W. Fostic

AT THE GOING DOWN OF THE
SUN AND IN THE MORNING
WE WILL REMEMBER HIM

Michael J. Hosier

EVEN HIS SAD THOUGHTS
LEAPT AND SHONE

Maurice L. Jensen

AT THE GOING DOWN OF THE
SUN AND IN THE MORNING
WE WILL REMEMBER THEM

A flight of nineteen AT-6s left Terrell for a cross-country flight to Miami, Oklahoma. The weather deteriorated and an attempt was made to recall the aircraft. Fourteen planes returned to Terrell, two planes reached Miami, one plane made a forced landing in Oklahoma, and two planes crashed in the Kiamichi mountains near Moyers, Oklahoma.

September 17, 1943
Kenneth W. Coaster

GOD'S GREATEST GIFT
REMEMBRANCE

M. B. McDonald, Instructor
Coaster ran out of fuel and landed three miles southwest of Waxahachie and called the Terrell airfield. McDonald brought fuel

to the site. Both Coaster and McDonald were killed when the aircraft failed to clear the trees at the end of the field on takeoff.

November 27, 1943
M. W. A. Williamson

A DEARLY LOVED SON
AND BROTHER
UNTIL WE MEET AGAIN
REST IN PEACE

Howard W. Perry, United States Army Air Force
Cliffard A. Levan, Instructor
Two aircraft collided in midair at 10:00 in the morning two miles from the Terrell airfield.

February 7, 1945
H. Gilbert Slocock

SON OF HAROLD AND
LILLY SLOCOCK
I THANK MY GOD FOR EVERY
REMEMBRANCE OF THEE

The only student to die of natural causes, Slocock had been in Terrell only a few weeks when he became ill. He died in the army hospital at Majors Field in Greenville. The medical officer listed the cause of death as tuberculosis.

September 3, 1945
Thomas S. Beedie

AS LONG AS LIFE
AND MEMORY LAST
WE WILL REMEMBER THEE

Raymond B. Botcher

SLEEP ON BELOVED
TAKE THY REST
WE LOVED THEE WELL BUT
JESUS LOVED THEE BEST

The AT-6 crashed into Lake Travis near Austin during a cross-country flight from San Marcos, Texas. The crash occurred one week before the school closed.

APPENDIX B

THE AT-6 INCIDENT

Hugh Morgan's book *By the Seat of Your Pants* has an interesting story on pages 115 and 116. According to Morgan, "Just hours before the arrival of the first course a potential crisis arose which was only averted by the inspirationally quick thinking of Wg Cdr Hilton." The civilian instructors had been to an RAF refresher course in Canada and the instructors there had very negative comments about the AT-6. "The aircraft apparently had an enormous number of vices. . . . it had an unfortunate tendency to fail to recover from a flat spin and ground loop when taxiing, etc." Hilton, according to Morgan, "Strode out to the nearest readily flyable AT6A, took off, and proceeded to put the aircraft through an imaginative aerobatic routine." Morgan concludes that No.1 BFTS never again received any complaints from the instructors regarding the suitability of the AT-6.

This is a great story and it has been repeated in other sources. It reads like a Hollywood movie script. The basis for the story is found in ORB dated June 14, 1941, and the writer (probably Flight Lieutenant Palmer since he was the administrative officer) readily admits this portion of the ORB had been written twenty-one months after the fact from the memory of others (Palmer did not arrive in Dallas until six weeks after the incident as described by Morgan).

There are several problems with this story. It is highly unlikely that Hilton actually performed an aerobatic routine including flat spins over Dallas Love Field, even though Palmer did use the term "demonstrate" in his description of the incident. The Operations Record Book (ORB) states the instructors attended the refresher course at Randolph Field in San Antonio, not Canada. Another point is the availability of the AT-6 at this time.

The record is clear that no aircraft or equipment had been delivered to Dallas Love Field before the first class arrived on June 2, 1941. The first Stearman PT-18s did not arrive in Dallas until four days later, on June 6, 1941. There would have been no reason for AT-6s to be at Dallas Aviation School on the first of June since Course 1 would not progress to advanced training for another four months and Major Long's contract with the army covered primary training only. Morgan states that Hilton went to the "nearest readily flyable AT-6" which indicates there must have been several on the flight line. The AT-6 was in short supply in June 1941. It is doubtful that a line of AT-6s would have been sitting in front of the Dallas Aviation School at Love Field on June 1, 1941. According to the Operations Record Book, the first five AT-6s arrived in Terrell on September 27, 1941. This would be exactly right for Course 1 to begin advanced training.

Early AT-6s did have a problem with spinning. Both the army and the RAF tested the aircraft extensively and prohibited spins until modifications to the vertical stabilizer attachments had been made (Palmer covers this point in the ORB). Morgan probably embellished a story that had some basis in truth. A discussion of the AT-6 probably did come up, but in late September, not early June as Morgan relates, and after the instructors went to San Antonio, not Canada. The episode likely occurred in Terrell (where a demonstration of the aircraft is more plausible than over Love Field). Hilton did praise the aircraft's good qualities and did help allay the Terrell instructors' concerns about the new trainer, but not in the overly dramatic Hollywood style described by Morgan.

Appendix C

We're the Boys of No. 1 BFTS

We're the Boys of No. 1 BFTS,
To our country's call we bravely answered "yes";
Crossing oceans at our peril, we have landed here in Terrell,
And how Texas first affects us we will leave you all to guess:
And though flying is the thing we're here to do,
We don't forget we're propaganda too;
So 'neath starry-spangled banners we're so careful of our manners,
We're the Boys of No. 1 BFTS,
Oh yes!
The British Boys of 1 BFTS

We're the Boys of No. 1 BFTS
And the Kaufman County Airport's our address;
It's a quiet little spot on down amongst the fields of cotton
But we're never quite forgotten by the public or the Press;
And when we're tired of doing rolls and lazy eights
We tramp into the town and look for dates;
And if girls are coy or callous, well, we thumb our way to Dallas,
We're the Boys of No. 1 BFTS
Oh yes!
The British Boys of 1 BFTS

We're the Boys of No. 1 BFTS
Our instructors give us trouble, we confess;
For their fire we are the fuel, when they take us up for dual
Their remarks are something cruel—still we're learning none the
    less;
And there's a photograph on ev'ry locker door
Of mother—or of Dorothy Lamour;
And often you are able to see lots of Betty Grable
With the Boys of No. 1 BFTS
 Oh yes!
The British Boys of 1 BFTS

We're the Boys of No. 1 BFTS
And our very grateful thanks we must express;
For though we're now in clover it will very soon be over,
We shall see the Cliffs of Dover and be clearing up the mess;
But when we've finished off the War and seen it through
We shall think of Terrell, Texas, and of you;
And though sea and sky may hide you they never can divide you
From the Boys of No. 1 BFTS
Oh yes!
The British Boys of 1 BFTS.

BIBLIOGRAPHY

I. Primary Sources

A. Archive Records

United Kingdom.

"Permanent Historical Record, Royal Air Force Operations Record Book, Form 540, Headquarters Air Historical Branch, Air Ministry, London, No.1 British Flying Training School, Texas, USA" AIR 29/625 and AIR 29/626. Located in the Public Record Office, London. This record is written in diary form and arranged by dates. Certain entries have letters, reports, appendixes, or other attachments.

"A System of Elementary Flying Training," Air Ministry, London, April 1941. This publication lists in detail the various steps and requirements for Reception Wing, ITW, preflight, and flight training for the RAF student pilot in 1941. Attached to the Operations Record Book, No.1 BFTS, described and located above.

"Notes for the Guidance of Aircrew Trainees Selected for Pilot and Observer Training at Certain Training Centers Overseas." Contains guidelines for British students entering the United States before December 7, 1941, and describes the students' status while in the United States. Attached to the Operations Record Book, No.1 BFTS, described and located above.

"Basic-Advanced Course Single Engine Syllabus (10 Weeks) For Use at British Flying Training Schools in U.S.A." This manual outlines several aspects of RAF flight training from instrument instruction, night flying, formation flying, ground school subjects. Located in Operations Record Book, No.1 BFTS, described and located above.

Microfilm file AIR 20/1387 and AIR 20/1388, Public Record Office, London. This file contains copies of correspondence from RAF officers in Washington, D.C., to officials at the Air Ministry in London concern-

ing training in the United States. Especially important is correspondence concerning proposed training prior to the United States' entry
into the war.

United States.

U.S. Air Force Historical Research Agency archives located at Maxwell
Air Force Base, Alabama. These records are contained on microfilm
roll A2281.

"History of the Dallas Aviation School, Love Field, Dallas, Texas, 1 July
1939 - 15 March 1941." Prepared by the Historical Section Army Air
Forces Central Flying Training Command, Randolph Field, Texas, 1
April 1945. Contained on microfilm roll A2281 located at the U.S. Air
Force Historical Research Agency archives at Maxwell Air Force base,
Alabama.

"History of the 321st Army Air Forces Flying Training Detachment, Terrell,
Texas." Reports of the army base unit assigned to No.1 BFTS, located
in Maxwell, microfilm roll A2281. These reports are arranged by date
and are either bi-monthly or quarterly.

"History of the 2564th Army Air Force Base Unit." This is a continuation
of the previous record after the unit had been redesignated. Located
on the same microfilm roll A2281.

B. Interviews

Baxter, Pauline (Bond). Interview by author. Kaufman, Texas, August 17,
2000.

Brewer, Virginia. Phone interview with author. October 8, 1993. Interview by author. Canton, Texas, September 10, 2000.

Brookover, Bill. Interview by author. Granbury, Texas, January 9, 2000.

Brown, Ben. Phone interview with author. February 12, 2000.

Flenniken, Ray. Interview by author. Arlington, Texas, April, 28, 2000.

Gill, Eric. Interview by author. Dallas, Texas, September 11, 2000.

Howell, Jane. Phone interview with author. December 18, 2000.

Krieger, Marvin. Interview by author. Dallas, Texas, February 21, 2000.

Madgwick, Henry. Interviews by author. Terrell, Texas, August 10, 1993,
and April 20, 2000.

Ridge, Arthur. Interviews by author. Terrell, Texas, January 29, 2000, and
Dallas, Texas, February 21, 2000.

C. Published Primary Sources

"Detached Flight" volumes I - VI published by the Terrell Aviation School, Terrell, Texas. Volumes III - VI on file in the Terrell Public Library. Volumes I and II are on microfilm roll A2281 in the U. S. Air Force archives located at Maxwell Air Force Base, Alabama.

British Air Ministry, "Flying Training, 1939-1945, vol I: Policy and Planning." A.H.B. Air Publication 3233, 1952.

D. Contemporary Journal and Magazine Articles 1940s

Forester, C. S. "The Truth About Our English Allies." *Look* (July 24, 1942): 11-13.

Garrod, , A. G. R. "Training and Manpower." *Flying* (September 1942): 107-10, 215-16.

Murphy, Mark. "Journey from Moncton." *New Yorker* (October 30, 1943): 46-54, 57-59.

Palmer, M. W. "British Flying Training Schools in America." *Transatlantic* (April 1945): 23-27.

_____. "Open Letter to a U/T Pilot." *RAF Journal* (September 1944).

"Pilots For Britain." *Time* (November 10, 1941): 56.

"RAF in the USA." *Scholastic, the American High School Weekly* (March 2-7, 1942): 28-30.

Steward, Davenport. "As the English See Us: John Bull Explains the American Way to the RAF Abroad." *Saturday Evening Post* (October 11, 1941): 24-25, 96.

E. Newspapers

Austin American Statesman
Dallas Morning News
Fort Worth Star Telegram
Houston Chronicle
New York Times
The Daily Times Herald (Dallas)
Terrell Daily Tribune
Waco Times Herald

F. Unpublished Papers and Manuscripts

Allam, A. J. "Into the Wild Blue Yonder," 1979.

Brewer, Virginia. "RAF Cemetery, Terrell, Texas," June 1991.

Guinn, Gilbert S. "BFTS No. 1, The Influence of Events."

———. Compilation of recollections by former students.

Madgwick, Henry C. Untitled, December 1997.

Rattan, Oklahoma, elementary school sixth grade reading project 1997-98, "AT-6s Crash Near Moyers During WW II", 1999.

G. Letters

Allam, A. J. Letters to author, Nov. 30, 1999 and January 12, 2000.

Ballance, Paul. Letter to author, January 19, 1994.

Bramson, Allan. Letters to author, July 29, 1994 and May 27, 2000.

Forteith, Jim. Letter to author, January 20, 2000.

Guinn, Gilbert S. Letter to author, November 3, 2002.

Stebbings, Don. Letter to author, November 8, 1993.

II. Secondary Sources

A. Books

Arnold, H. H. *Global Mission.* New York: Harper and Brothers, 1949.

Cearley, George W. *A Pictorial History of Airline Service at Dallas Love Field.* Dallas: np, 1989.

Churchill, Winston S. *The Second World War: Their Finest Hour.* Boston: Houghton Mifflin Company, 1949.

_____. *The Second World War: The Hinge of Fate.* Boston: Houghton Mifflin Company, 1950.

_____. *The Second World War: The Grand Alliance.* Boston: Houghton Mifflin Company, 1950.

Clark, Alan. *Barbarossa: The Russian-German Conflict, 1941-45.* New York: Morrow, 1965.

Coffey, Thomas M. *Hap: The Story of the U.S. Air Force and the Man Who Built It, General Henry H. "Hap" Arnold.* New York: The Viking Press, 1982.

Craven, Wesley Frank and James Lea Cate, eds. *The Army Airforces in World War II, Vol. I: Plans and Early Operations January 1939 to August 1942.* Chicago: University of Chicago Press, 1948.

Dupuy, Trevor N., Curt Johnson, and David L. Bongard. *The Harper Encyclopedia of Military Biography.* New York: HarperCollins Publishers, 1992.

Forrester, Larry. *Fly for Your Life: The Story of R. R. Stanford Tuck, D.S.O., D.F.C., and Two Bars.* New York: Bantam Books, 1978.

Gentile, Gary. *Track of the Grey Wolf: U-boat Warfare on the U.S. Eastern Seaboard 1942-1945*. New York: Avon Books, 1989.

Golley, John. *Aircrew Unlimited: the Commonwealth Air Training Plan during World War II*. London: Patrick Stephens Ltd., 1993.

Green, William. *Famous Fighters of the Second World War*. New York: Hanover House, 1958.

Hynes, Samuel. *Flights of Passage*. New York: Simon and Schuster Inc., 1988.

James, Joe. *Teacher Wore a Parachute*. New York: A. S. Barnes and Company, 1966.

Jane's Fighting Aircraft of World War II. London: Jane's Publishing Company, 1946; Reprint, Singapore: Random House, 1994.

Kohn, Leo J. *The Story of the Texan*. Appleton, Wisconsin: Aviation Publications, 1989.

Largent, Will. *RAF Wings over Florida: Memories of World War II British Air Cadets*. West Lafayette, Indiana: Purdue University Press, 2000.

Lukacs, John. *Five Days in London:May 1940*. New Haven: Yale University Press, 1999.

Manchester, William. *The Last Lion: Winston Spencer Churchill, Alone 1932-1940*. Boston: Little, Brown and Company, 1988.

Messenger, Charles. *The Chronological Atlas of World War Two*. New York: Macmillan Publishing Company, 1989.

Morgan, Hugh. *By the Seat of Your Pants*. Cowden, Kent, Great Britain: Newton Publishers, 1990.

Reynolds, Clark G. *Admiral John H. Towers: The Struggle for Naval Air Supremacy*. Annapolis, Maryland: Naval Institute Press, 1991.

Richards, Denis. *Royal Air Force 1939-1945, Vol. I: The Fight at Odds*. London: Her Majesty's Stationery Office, 1953.

Round, Thomas. *A Wand'ring Mistrel, I: The Autobiography of Thomas Round*. Lancaster, Great Britain: Carnegie Publishing Ltd, 2002.

Stoltz, Jack. *Terrell Texas 1873-1973: From Open Country to Modern City*. San Antonio: The Naylor Company, 1973.

Terrell Centennial 1873-1973. Undated essays arranged by the Terrell Historical Society, 1973.

Townsend, Peter. *Duel of Eagles*. New York: Simon and Schuster, 1971.

Terraine, John. *A Time for Courage: The Royal Air Force in the European War, 1939-1945*. New York: Macmillan, 1985.

Wiener, Willard. *Two Hundred Thousand Flyers, the Story of the Civilian-AAF Pilot Training Program.* Washington: The Infantry Journal, 1945.

Wiggins, Melanie. *Torpedoes in the Gulf: Galveston and the U-Boats, 1942-1943.* College Station, Texas: Texas A&M University Press, 1995.

Wrynn, Dennis V. *Detroit Goes to War: The American Automobile Industry in World War II.* Osceola, Wisconsin: Motorbooks International, 1993.

B. Magazine and Journal Articles

Abbott, J. L. "Forever England." *Air Power History* (Summer 1995): 20-22.

Bowyer, Chaz. "Bomber VC, the Story of Flt Sgt A.L. Aaron, VC, DFM." *Aircraft Illustrated Extra, Bombers of World War II* (no. 10): 34-39.

Brown, Ben L. "The RAF in Texas." *Friends Journal* 15 (Summer 1992): 18-22.

_____. "When the RAF Invaded Texas!" *Air Classics* (June 2000): 21-23, 60-63; (July 2000): 24-32.

Guinn, Gilbert S. "British Aircrew Training in the United States 1941-1945." *Air Power History* (Summer 1995): 5-19.

Peeters, Tracy. "The Brits Are Back!" *Texas Highways* (October 1991): 21-25.

Schirmer, Robert F. "AAC & AAF Civil Primary Flying Schools 1939-1945, Part VII Dallas Primary." *Journal, American Aviation Historical Society* (Fall 1992): 215-22.

INDEX

LaVergne, TN USA
14 October 2009
160835LV00003B/2/P